ART AND HISTORY

ASSISI

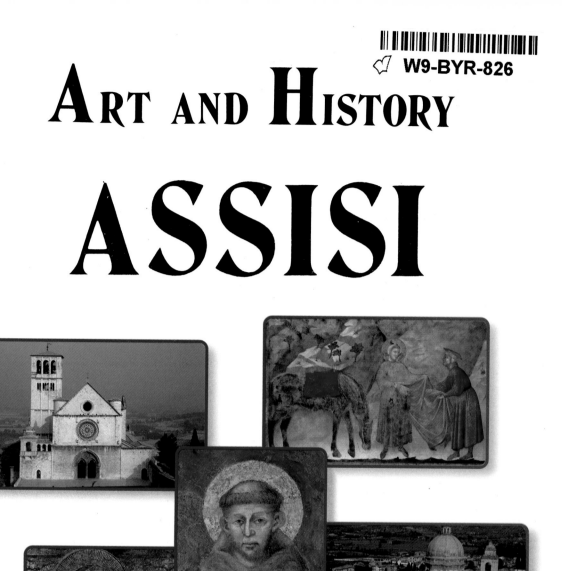

Text
R. P. Nicola Giandomenico

© Copyright by CASA EDITRICE BONECHI
Via Cairoli 18b - 50131 Florence, Italy
Tel. +39 055576841 - Fax +39 0555000766
E-mail: bonechi@bonechi.it - Internet: www.bonechi.it

Project and editorial conception: Casa Editrice Bonechi
Publication Manager: Monica Bonechi
Graphic design: Marco Bonechi, Monica Bonechi *and* Serena de Leonardis
Picture research: Serena de Leonardis *and* Marco Bonechi
Editing: Patrizia Fabbri
Make-up: Federica Balloni
Cover: Manuela Ranfagni
Text: R.P. Nicola Giandomenico
Drawing: Stefano Benini
Map of Assisi: Filippo Topi

Printed in Italy by Centro Stampa Editoriale Bonechi.

Photographs from the archives of Casa Editrice Bonechi *taken by*
R.P. Gerhard Ruf, Paolo Giambone, MSA, Marco Bonechi.

Other contributors:
Andrea Pistolesi: *pages 74 above left, 75, 79 below right and left, 101 below, 120 above right and below;*
Ghigo Roli: *pages 11-16, 23, 28, 30-31, 36, 49-68, 72-73, 100 below right and left, 101 above right, 119, 124-125*
and right flap, above right and below left and right.
Massimo Sestini Fotogiornalismo: *three photographs above left on the right flap.*

ISBN 978-88-476-0415-5

A 10 9 8 7 6 5 4 3 2 1

Panorama of Assisi.

INTRODUCTION

The enchanting town of Assisi, packed with history and of universal religious appeal, is situated in the green heart of Umbria.

Spread out over the northwestern slopes of Mt. Subasio (one of the mountains in the Apennine chain), it dominates the plain below, named after Spoleto, that extends up to the hills on which the city of Perugia lies. The sweeping views encompass the fertile countryside on the plain and the dense woods towards the mountain. Enveloped in the diaphanous light of the Umbrian skies, the town with its stone houses arranged in tiers rises up over the valley like a vision of peace, a synthesis of the marvels of the land and the genius of man.

On the northwest, the Basilica of San Francesco and the Convent loom large. In the center and to the east the campanili and the tower of the City Hall reach skywards while the reddish roofs and the rustic masonry of the houses are an integral part of this marvelous but simple allover view.

Assisi's charm lies in its beauty... in the beauty of the way in which the architecture reflects life, in its town plan, in its sanctuaries, in the paintings by the greatest 13th and 14th-century masters. Just being there is an experience that will sweetly linger in your memory, for the city is a place of calm and tranquillity, a spiritual oasis in which to recover one's peace of mind, a sacred space in which to pause and spiritually recuperate from the stress of daily life and to be infused with new spiritual energy to help us face the trials and tribulations of daily life.

The geographical site, at the outlet of river valleys and traffic routes and with a mountain hinterland, combined with the prominent role it plays in the field of religion in international circles, makes Assisi timeless and universal, a reality above and beyond the contingent vicissitudes of the modern world, with an ideal aura in which to rediscover spiritual values.

Very little exists in the way of documentary tradition for the name «Assisi». The origins of the city are lost in times immemorial. Legend narrates that it was built by Asio, brother of the queen of Troy. Most scholars think the name derives from «acu», or east, since it was the city to the east of Perugia. For Dante the name Assisi come from the Latin «ascendere» with reference to the great light it emanated thanks to the figure of St. Francis.

The city of Assisi dates back to pre-Roman times. It was an important center, inhabited by the Umbri, and then by the Romans, who conferred important privileges on the city.

What we know of ancient Assisi is due above all to archaeological remains, primarily architecture, rather than to historical or literary sources. The latter in particular say pratically nothing about the city. The first time Assisi is directly mentioned is by Propertius, the famous Latin poet who came from there. The name of Assisi does not appear again until the period of the Goths and the struggles between Goths and Byzantines.

3

In the third century A.D., the Christian faith was brought to Assisi by Bishop Rufinus.

After the fall of the Roman Empire, Assisi was besieged and laid waste more than once, invaded by Totila's Lombards and by the Carolingians, annexed by the Duchy of Spoleto. Between the year 1000 and the 14th century, the city acquired its present aspect and enjoyed a marvelous period of life as a free commune. In the 14th-16th centuries it was rent by intestine struggles and bitter wars with the neighboring Umbrian cities. From the 16th century on until 1860 it was part of the Papal States, a period of peace that was also marked by centuries of «deep lethargy».

With the advent of the 20th century, Assisi became extremely active in the fields of culture, civil initiatives and religion.

At present the commune numbers around 25,000 inhabitants, of which only 6,000 reside in the city center, and it is an episcopal see. But the greatness of Assisi depends on the fact that it was the birthplace of Francis and Clare and of the whole movement that began with them.

Opposite page, above: the parchment of the Order, drawn up by Saint Francis, of which it is possible to admire on this page, below, a detail and the papal seal of Honorious III, affixed to confirm his approval.

Opposite page, below: the Blessing for Brother Leone, a parchment preserved in the Chapel of Relics of the Lower Basilica.

The tunic of Saint Francis.

SILENT WITNESSES

Assisi and St. Francis are one and the same thing. There is no other place where the spirit and the spirituality of the Saint are so omnipresent as Assisi. So many of the places speak to us of him: the little church of San Damiano, the Hermitage of the Carceri, the cathedral of San Rufino, the hovel of Rivotorto, the Porziuncola, the basilica of Santa Chiara, the Bishop's palace, the Basilica complex erected in his honor. In the Chapel of the Relics, in the Lower Church (of San Francesco), various *silent witnesses* are preserved which are tangible living signs of the Saint, historical documents that are part of his life and eloquent expressions of his saintliness. First and foremost are: the Rule, the tunic, the blessing to Fra Leone written in his own hand.

The Rule. Three years before Francis died Pope Honorius III granted him written approval of the Order with the Papal Bull «*Solet Annuere*» of November 29, 1223. This is the Rule composed by St. Francis with the aid of Cardinal Ugolino (later Gregory IX) and some of the friars, written on parchment with a curial calligraphy and with the papal seal. The text consists of twelve chapters and begins with these words: «The Rule and the life of the Brothers Minor is as follows: that is observation of the Holy Gospels of our Lord Jesus Christ, living in obedience, with nothing of their own, and in chastity».

The tunic. The most eloquent evidence of the way in which Francis lived is this tunic in rough sheep's wool, a coarse fabric with white and black threads, greyish in color. It is the expression of his detachment from worldly things and clearly indicates the Saint's social preferences.

The Blessing to Fra Leone written in his own hand. It was written by St. Francis on the mount in La Verna for Fra Leone, his confessor-secretary and nurse, in September 1224, immediately after receiving the stigmata. On one side is the blessing taken from the Book of Numbers in the Bible, on the other the prayer of «Praise to the Lord». The parchment is wrinkled and spotted because Fra Leone carried it on his person for all of forty-seven years, from 1224 to 1271, when on his deathbed he left it to the Holy Monastery.

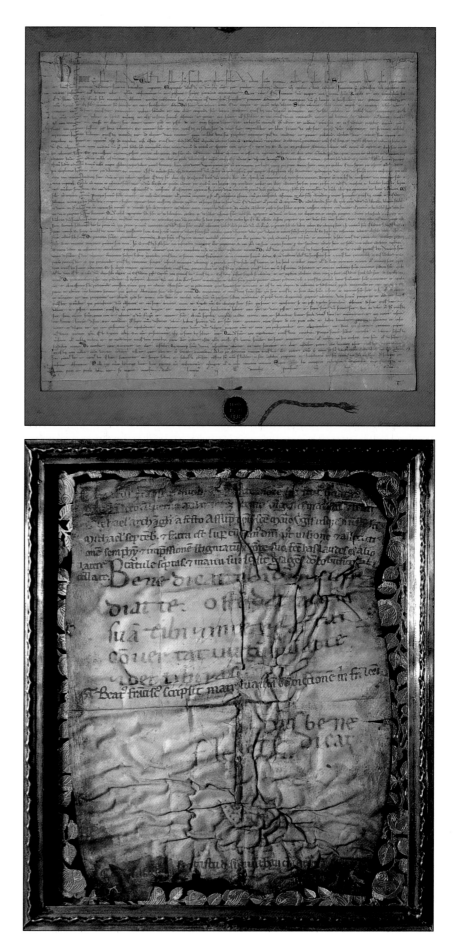

SACRO CONVENTO

Those who arrive in Assisi first see the basilica complex from the lower square with its arcades built around 1467 – an entrance which invites one to concentrate on the encounter with St. Francis. The present aspect of the porch dates to 1487, with the inscription which mentions the date and General Francesco Sansone who was responsible for the construction. The portal however dates to the 14th century and repeats, in a mature Gothic version, the scheme of the portal of the Upper Church. A rose window is included in the upper part.

The «church-mausoleum» which contains and honors the body of the Saint is surrounded by the living quarters of the friars. Since the Franciscans could own no property, Pope Gregory IX, in name of the Holy See, became patron and owner of both the Church and the Convent. As a result, while the original convent, built parallel to the church itself, was meant to house the community of friars to whom the basilica was entrusted, it was officially known as the Papal Palace! And various popes have stayed there.

There was mention of the first nucleus of the Convent as early as 1230 when there was a General Chapter of the Order in Assisi. The residential area for the pope was in part finished, on the north side, in 1235. Gregory IX was the first to live there.

The original rooms of the friary, built of the same stone as the Basilica, are in Romanesque style. Their simplicity and humility is intact and the love of poverty shines forth in all its splendor.

In 1363 the place was first called «Sacro Convento», in other words not just any convent, but the convent of convents, the convent of the church defined by the Pontiffs as the «head and mother» of the entire Franciscan order. The present building was terminated in the course of two centuries, with works of consolidation and modernization, and took on its final form at the end of the 15th century.

In the 14th century the first enlargement – towards the plain – took place, built by Niccolò da Bettona at the behest of Cardinal E. Albornoz. In the 15th century Pope Sixtus IV had the whole side facing the plain reinforced by a sustaining structure which includes fifty-four arches, twenty-seven of which support the lower square of the Basilica and twenty-seven the Convent. He also had a large buttress built north of the Basilica and enlarged the entire zone.

Set on a slope as it is, this imposing complex looks like a fortress, almost as if it were meant to defend the church itself and the body of the Saint. It is the cradle of Franciscan ideals. The Conventual Friars Minor who live there are intimately committed to the evangelical ideals St. Francis required of his friars, and they do all they can to give concrete evidence of brotherhood by dedicating themselves to an intense life of prayer.

Some of the rooms are destined for meditation and prayer. Outstanding in this sense is the **14th-century portico** in Romanesque style, with a perfect flight of Gothic arches, and an enchanting panorama that includes the Umbrian valley in its sweep.

An aerial view which clearly shows the architectural structure of the complex of the Basilicas and Sacro Convento of Assisi.

THE BASILICAS

The basilica complex of Assisi is famous the world over for its marvelous synthesis of architecture, painting, and spirituality. It is the prototype of Italian Gothic art. Inside it houses the frescoes of the greatest painters of the 13th and 14th centuries. Thanks to the presence of St. Francis it emanates a unique spiritual attraction. The entire building obeys precise criteria.

The daring unusual structure envisioned by Brother Elias was from the beginning in the form of a church with two superposed levels which would house the mortal remains of St. Francis and be a sure harbor of faith for all the world, a place suitable for prayer, an occasion for analysis and comparison. In other words not a convent church as abbey but a mausoleum church, which was to be in the form of the tau cross, so dear to St. Francis, and the biblical sign of salvation. The Lower Church, crypt and massive foundations for the entire building, destined to receive the sarcophagus of the Saint, was intended to be sober, immersed in shadows, with a distinctly Romanesque architecture. The Upper Church, to the contrary, was to be luminous, spacious, the expression of joy and grace. And it is here that the French Gothic attained its maximum expression.

The first documents relative to the construction date to March 12, 1228, with the donation of a piece of land by Simone di Pucciarello for the erection of a building «*pro beatissimo corpore Sancti Francisci*». The original area was enlarged with another donation on July 31, 1239, which already makes reference to an «*ecclesia Sancti Francisci*», and was concluded with the purchase of the land already occupied by the friars during the works, in December 1246. The choice of the site significantly fell on a steep wooded area, outside the city, known as «Colle dell'Inferno» (Hell Hill) where the death sentences were carried out. But before long this hilly site came to be known as «Colle del Paradiso» thanks to the presence of the body of the Saint.

Work was coordinated by Brother Elias and directed by Comacine masters. On July 16, 1228, Pope Gregory IX canonized St. Francis and the day after he laid the first stone. The Lower Church was ready by 1230 and on May 25th of that year the body of the Saint was solemnly transferred from the Chapel of San Giorgio. And it was once more Pope Gregory who with his brief «*Is qui*» on April

The complex of the Sacro Convento of Assisi with the imposing arcaded buttresses dating to the 15th century.

On the following pages: the Basilica of San Francesco at the back of the Piazza Inferiore.

22, 1230 proclaimed the church «head and mother» of the Franciscan Order, setting it under his protection.
The basic wall structures of the bell tower and of the Upper Church were terminated in 1236. When he stopped in Assisi on his return from Avignon in 1253 Pope Innocent IV in person consecrated the Upper Church. Further works in the last quarter of the 13th century were concerned essentially with the entrance and the chapels of the Lower Church. All the rest remained as it was. Only the marvelous bell tower, in Lombard Romanesque style and sixty meters high, lost its spire in 1530 when it was struck by lightning.
The greatest painters of the time were immediately called in for the pictorial decoration: the first to arrive was Giunta Pisano, then Cimabue, the Roman masters with Cavallini and Torriti, then Giotto, Simone Martini, the Lorenzetti brothers... with a throng of followers. Other artists also came later, such as Puccio Capanna, A. da Bologna. In the 16th and 17th centuries, Dono Doni, C. Sermei, G. Martelli, G. Giorgetti frescoed the remaining walls. Even though their works are real masterpieces, they are overshadowed by the great names who preceded them.

Two views of the south side of the Basilica of San Francesco with the entrance portal to the Lower Church.

On the following two pages: an all-over view of the Lower Church, characterized by the calligraphic decorations on the arches of the vaulting.

LOWER CHURCH

Round-headed arches divide the single nave of the Lower Church into four bays with cross vaulting. The powerful ribs spring from the short semicircular pilasters without base. The arms of the transept have barrel vaults. Upon entering, attention is immediately drawn to the *High Altar* which is at the center of the crossing over the Tomb of the Saint. It is the work of the Cosmati masters and has twenty small Gothic columns with capitals and arches decorated with mosaics. The altar table is a single slab of marble (3.80×1.80 m). Glancing up over the altar one sees the four allegorical paintings set into the four sections of the vault. According to Vasari, they were frescoed by Giotto. Currently critics attribute them to an unknown painter conventionally known as «Maestro delle Vele». They depict the exaltation of the Glory of St. Francis through his three vows of poverty, chastity, obedience. Behind the altar are wooden *choir stalls* (1468-1471), constructed by Apollonio Petrocchi da Ripatransone with the aid of various masters. It is an excellent example of carving with various figures and plant motifs. An irregular octagon in shape, the upper tier has thirty-one seats, and the lower twenty stools, enclosed by a balustrade of small columns supporting interlacing inlaid arches.

The famous Crucifixion by Giotto in the Lower Basilica.

Opposite, the allegory of Obedience (above) and the Triumph, with Francis on the throne, frescoed on the ribbed vault of the cross.

The allegory of Chastity, a fresco by the "Maestro delle Vele", on the vault section near the right transept. It is possible to recognize, from left to right, Dante Alighieri, Fra' Giovanni di Muro and St. Clare in the presence of St. Francis, the personification of Chastity (on the central tower) and, to the right, the Expulsion of the Demons.

CIMABUE'S MAESTA

St. Francis appears ninety-two times in the art works of the Basilica: sixty-five times in fresco, sixteen on glass, six in wood, two in stone and terracotta, once in mosaic and twice in bronze.

Cimabue arrived in Assisi around 1280 and the marvelous masterpiece in the right transept of the Lower Church is by his hand: the Madonna, sweet and melancholy, seated on a regal throne, is flanked by four angels. The figure of St. Anthony may have been on the left but it was eliminated at the beginning of the 14th century to make room for the Giottesque Crucifixion. On the right is the famous portrait of the *Poverello*, which corresponds to the description left by Francis' first biographer, Tom-

maso da Celano:

«...Rather small of stature, his head regular and round, with an oval forward-looking face, his forehead low and smooth, his dark eyes of moderate size and candid, his hair dark, straight eyebrows, a nose as it should be, thin and straight, small ears close to the head, his temples smooth, speech that was mild, fiery and penetrating, a powerful voice, sweet and harmonious, his teeth all white and close together, small thin lips, his beard dark and rather sparse, straight shoulders, slender hands with long fingers and nails, slender legs, small feet, a delicate complexion; thin, with a rough tunic, in need of little sleep, most generous. In his great humility he showed himself good and understanding with all, wisely conforming to the manners of others. Truly among saints he was the saintliest, among sinners as one of themselves».

RIGHT TRANSEPT OF THE LOWER CHURCH

Nativity

There is an extensive cycle of frescoes (ca. 1310) in the right arm of the transept of the Lower Church. The cycle is dedicated to the infancy of Christ and was painted by the school of Giotto, following the story as told in the Gospels and in the apocryphal writings.

The scene of the *Nativity* is particularly vivacious and expressive. The hut stands by itself with the mountain rising up in the background. The star peeks out between two peaks. The angels have diverse functions: above the hut

they sing «Glory to God in the Highest», one at the side speaks to the shepherds, others in the hut worship the Christ Child. The ox and the ass tenderly observe Jesus, the sheep and rams seem to participate in the event.

Joseph is thoughtful. The Madonna is seated on the ground holding the Child. Jesus appears twice in the scene, once here standing on His mother's knees, and further down in the arms of a woman who is touching His nose as she tries to make Him smile while another woman prepares His bath. Each figure seems to live in a world of its own and as a result the scene seems fragmentary.

Flight to Egypt

A lyrical, relaxed narrative scene. Only the essential figures are shown and a wealth of details enlivens the story.

The landscape is harsh, steely. Nature appears centered around the figures. The mountains seem to tend towards those who are crossing through; the bushes, trees, the palm lean towards Jesus.

Joseph, tired and bent, leads the way, pulling along the beast of burden and turning his head to look at Mary. Over his left shoulder he holds a short stick with a bundle hanging from it.

Mary, seated on her mount, tightly clasps the Child, supported by a sash around her neck, and seems to be encouraging Joseph. Behind are two other figures. The young man seems to be inciting the ass to hurry on. Above are two angels: one looks ahead searching the horizon, the other looks backwards, almost as if fearing the arrival of Herod.

Slaughter of the Innocents

An extraordinary group and a highly dramatic scene with a wide variety of postures and expressions of grief on the part of the mothers of the babes.

From the top of a tower, Herod, together with the priests, orders all the newborn babes in the region killed in his attempt to eliminate the new king. The bodies pile up in the center of the square. The soldiers, hesitant and sad because of their task, close all the entrances. The surrounding houses also seem to participate in the scene, facing onto the square with their empty windows and silhouetted against the luminous blue as pure as the souls of the murdered babes. The two horses also seem to be looking towards Herod, the cause of all this grief.

Polyptych by Simone Martini

Under the miracle of the boy of Suessa, against the wall of the Chapel of S. Nicola, not far above ground level, is a small painted gallery of saints, divided into five compartments by slender twisted columns. Each compartment contains a saint, and is decorated with gold impressions. These frescoes reveal the characteristics of Sienese painting: harmonious lines, luminous colours, the aristocratic features of the figures, almond-shaped eyes. The painter was Simone Martini (ca 1317). It is almost a polyptych with eight figures of saints (St. Francis, St. Louis of Toulouse, St. Elisabeth of Hungary, St. Clare, St. Elzeario, the Madonna and Child between two crowned saints) who seem to be communicating with the people.

Francis to Death

To the right of the choir there is a staircase that leads to the cloister of Sixtus IV. With its interlacing pointed arches decorated on the exterior with imitation Cosmati work, it dates to the early period of the construction of the Basilica and permitted the Pope, when he was in Assisi, to reach his private apartments.

At the top, on the right, is a fresco in the style of Giotto, apparently odd, but extremely didactic and catechistic. St. Francis with the stigmata, raises his right hand in sign of welcome and acceptance, and lays his left hand on a skeleton which is leaning against a wooden coffin and wearing a gold crown about to topple from its head.

There are two other frescoes on the adjacent walls in which St. Francis resuscitates two dead children: a little girl of Casa Sperelli and the boy of Suessa. The meaning is obvious: not only has St. Francis conquered death, but he considers death a friend and sister: «Praise... to the Lord, for our sister corporal death, from whom no living man can flee».

On the following pages: details of the extremely realistic and expressive portraits of the "Poverello" (St. Francis) and St. Clare.

LEFT TRANSEPT OF THE LOWER CHURCH

Hanging of Judas

To the left of the choir a staircase leads from the Lower Church to the cloister of Sixtus IV. Built shortly after the one on the right, it was meant to provide access to the monastery for the friars of the community. The structure is Gothic. A dramatic vision lies half hidden in the half light under a dark arch in the corner between the stairs and the wall. It is the macabre spectacle of Judas who is hanging himself. The fresco is attributed to Pietro Lorenzetti.

After the Crucifixion, the suicide of Judas was a recurrent theme in the sermons of the time, even though it was rarely depicted in the Passion cycles. Pietro Lorenzetti did, however, in an impressive scene that must have a precise meaning. Judas is shown hanging from a beam, dressed in green and with his abdomen slashed.

The picture of Judas the suicide has to be seen in relation to that of St. Francis who conquers death, shown in the corresponding area of the right transept. Judas hanged himself because he did not believe in the pardon and mercy of God. St. Francis opened himself to the grace of God by the «imitation of the Cross».

The frescoes in the two arms of the transept of the Lower Church show us St. Francis not as the *altar Christus* but as an exceptional teacher: as he who has achieved sainthood and who shows it to all Christians, through the way of obedience, penitence, imitation of Christ.

Washing of the Feet

While the figures are marvelously portrayed in all their details, the painter takes a few liberties in the setting of this Gospel tale. The episode takes place not in the cenaculum but in the nave of a Gothic church with cross vaulting scattered with gold stars. For some this is the Upper Church of Assisi.

The evangelical scene narrates of the dialogue between Jesus, who bends over to wash the feet of the apostles, and Peter, who first refused and then willingly accepted. The other apostles are seated around the spacious hall and turn naturally towards the main scene, interested in the dialogue. One of them is about to take off his shoes while Judas is off to one side and expresses his refusal with a gesture.

Crucifixion

The scene which occupies the second and third register of the eastern wall of the transept is truly unforgettable. Even though much of it has been damaged, the imposing *Crucifixion* is alive and palpitating, comprised of a mass of marvelous individual figures, each one perfectly finished, each one the leading actor in the drama. The taste for refinement and ornamental detail does not in the least diminish the religious intensity. To the contrary, this won-

derful fresco is a powerful invitation to an encounter with Christ on the cross. The three crosses, with their tormented bodies, are silhouetted against the deep blue sky. The angels, all different in expression and gesture, flutter around in anguish. This is the first time in the west that the thieves appear in a monumental composition. The crowd is the most important part: these carefully delineated sixty-five figures lend movement to the whole picture.

The soldiers casting lots for Christ's clothing were once at the foot of the cross. Part of the fresco was lost in 1617 when a marble altar dedicated to St. John the Baptist and

used for the exposition of the relics was set against the wall. It was removed in 1870.

In the early decades of the 14th century Siena exploded with artistic creativity and became one of the most important and qualified centers for the diffusion of the new western style known later as «Gothic». Its greatest representatives in the field of painting were Simone Martinii (1284-1344) and Pietro Lorenzetti (1280-1348). These two painters from Siena acquired such prestige at the beginning of the 14th century that they replaced Giotto and his workshop in the decoration of the Lower Church in Assisi.

Between 1310-1320, Pietro Lorenzetti, together with his brother Ambrogio and a group of pupils, frescoed the left sector of the Lower Church with scenes from the *Passion of Christ* and the *Life of St. Francis*.

These frescoes are imbued with drama and religious piety. The color is exceptionally vivid. Often the details are more interesting than the all-over scene (see, for instance, the details of the large scene of the *Crucifixion*).

Even though he was barely thirty, Pietro Lorenzetti was at the height of his expressive powers in the frescoes in Assisi and has bequeathed us with an intense and harmonious work of art.

Sunset Madonna

Another marvel by Lorenzetti, the stupendous Madonna and Child with St. Francis and St. John Evangelist on either side is commonly called the Sunset Madonna because the last light of the setting sun strikes the fresco. The picture was in a loggia and the balustrade formed the predella of an altar which no longer exists, with the portraits of the donors. The donor on the left and the end of St. Francis' arm have disappeared. The two saints are the same size, while the Virgin Mary, with the Child in her arms, is taller.

The freshness of the faces, the delicacy of the lines, the grace of the colors, the gold background make this fresco one of the best-known and most moving pictures in Italian art. It is the most enchanting work in the entire Basilica and makes an indelible impression on the visitor.

The Madonna and Child are talking and gesticulating. What are they talking about? The most popular version is that the Child is asking His mother who loved Him most and the Virgin points to St. Francis.

Entry of Christ into Jerusalem

The scene is full of light and exuberance. Jesus is seated on an ass, flanked by a colt. They are followed by the apostles, all with halos except Judas. Peter is in the foreground, next to Judas. The exulting crowd comes out of the city gates, carrying palms. On this side of the wall, on a hill with trees, two boys break off olive branches and cast them into the road. Even the birds over the gates seem to be rejoicing.

Jerusalem is seen as a splendid sumptuous city, with Gothic buildings climbing up the slope, and defended by crenellated walls. The architecture is of a Sienese type and emphasizes the colors and the figures. The walls of the houses and the towers are highly decorated.

Kiss of Judas

The scene takes place in the garden of olives. Judas is shown about to kiss Jesus, approaching Him and putting one hand on His breast. Jesus raises His head as if surprised and looks at him with diffidence. The apostles are about to flee, frightened by the arrival of the group of persons who intend to make their master prisoner. The last one turns back to observe the scene. Only Peter has stopped to talk with one of them. The chief priests and the elders can be clearly distinguished in the crowd, while the host of soldiers are all grouped together in the center in a blackish indistinct mass. In the Gospels the event took place at night. And Pietro Lorenzetti has frescoed a clear clear night. Some critics indeed have called it «the first night scene in Italian art». It is in fact a splendid night scene: starry sky, the moon setting behind the mountain, the trees clearly silhouetted, the pale white rocks. There is even a shooting star.

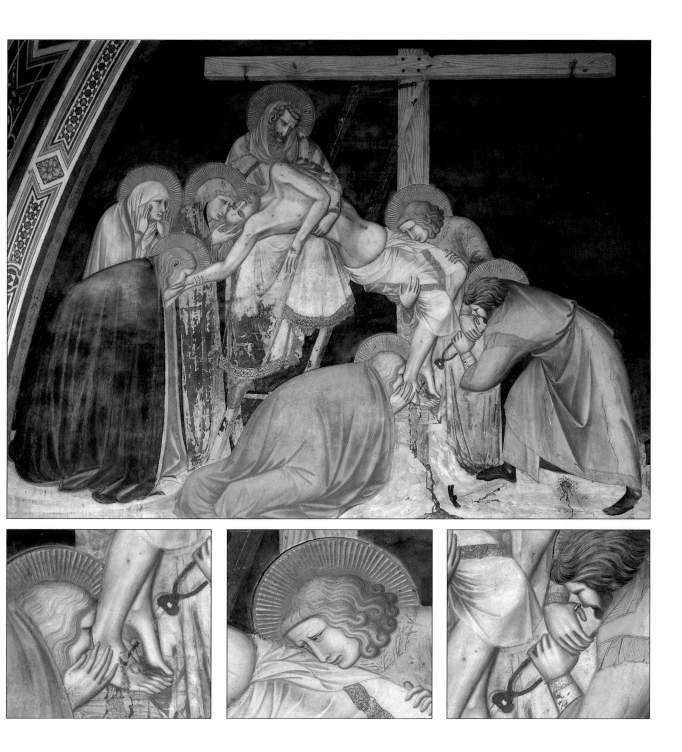

Deposition

On the left part of the entrance to the Chapel of St. John the Baptist, against an undecorated background, is the fresco of the *Deposition.*

The tau-shaped cross rises up bare against the empty background. Seven figures encircle the lifeless body of the Saviour, taken off the cross with his limbs dislocated and twisted, his head and arms dangling. All are bending over the inert body of Christ, to support it, to kiss it.

The lamentations of the pious women (Mary Magdalen, Mary of Cleophe and Mary of Jacob) express an insupportable grief. The Madonna brings her disconsolate face close to that of Jesus. John, petrified with grief, embraces the body of Christ «with eyes that are about to weep but will never weep, for his tears have turned to crystal, that is quartz in his eyes». Joseph of Arimathaea is offering his tomb for the burial. A man is removing the nails with pincers.

The group is almost in the shape of a pyramid. The individual figures are like the spokes of a wheel around Christ.

The gestures are essential and highly dramatic. Pietro Lorenzetti frescoed it in one of the high points of his life. Some critics have called this *Deposition* one of the finest expressions of the dramatic genius of Italian trecento painting.

31

SIMONE MARTINI:
THE CHAPEL OF SAN MARTINO

Simone Martini was born in Siena around 1284. When he was barely twenty he began his art apprenticeship in the circle of Duccio di Buoninsegna. He painted first in Siena and then in Assisi; later in Naples, Pisa, Siena, Orvieto. Around 1340 he moved to the papal court in Avignon where he died in July 1344. Between 1314-1318 he was in Assisi where he frescoed the chapel of St. Martin, eight paintings of *Saints* on the back wall of the right transept of the Lower Church, and prepared the cartoons for the stained-glass windows of the chapels of St. Martin and of St. Louis (now St. Stephen).

Esthetically these works are on a very high level. Each picture is a masterpiece, in which the feeling for line, the refined use of color, the delicacy of forms all come to the fore. The period in which the painter lived was characterized by a particularly European outlook and a transferral of cultures and his works reflect the mysticism and regal worldliness, the pomp of worldly life and severe spirituality, joy of life and adherence to exterior forms of magnificence typical of his times. All his figures move in a world of grace and gentility, of musical calm where sin and grief are intruders.

The Franciscan cardinal Gentile di Partino da Montefiore called Simone Martini to paint the Chapel of San Martino in Assisi. The results were the outstanding frescoes with a narration in which sweetness, finesse and grace are mingled. Many consider the chapel one of the sublime moments of 14th-century painting.

The Chapel of San Martino is the first chapel to the left in the nave of the Lower Church. It is a rectangular Gothic space, covered with a barrel vault and terminating in a spacious hexagonal apse with six ogive sectors in the vault separated by slender ribs. In each of the three central sections of the apse is a two-light window with deep-set splays. Red and white marble inlays form the dado of the walls, while the supporting columns are of red granite. The sections of the vault are painted in ultramarine blue with gold stars. The ribs are decorated with geometric designs.

There are eight *Saints* set full figure onto the under side of the entrance arch. They are arranged in pairs under pointed trilobate arches which spring from twisted columns: St. Catherine Martyr and Mary Magdalen; Francis and Anthony of Padua, Louis king of France and Louis of Toulouse; Clare of Assisi and Elisabeth of Hungary.

The ten *Scenes from the life of St. Martin* are arranged on the side walls and on the barrel vault. Each panel is separated from the one next to it by a frame with geometric design and four medallions with angelic busts at the corners. The inscriptions – now completely gone – which commented each episode were in the frames. From left to right the scenes represent: St. Martin dividing his cloak with a poor man; resuscitating a boy; attending the funeral of the Bishop of Tours; death and apotheosis of the Saint; honored by the Emperor Valentinian; renouncing the military career; Christ appearing to the Saint with the cloak he gave the poor man; Martin taking leave from St. Ilario; knighted by the Emperor Costanzo; assisted by the angels he celebrates holy mass.

Left: the magnificent central stained-glass window of the Chapel of San Martino on cartoons by Simone Martini. Facing page: St. Clare and St. Elisabeth frescoed by Simone Martini on the underside of the entrance arch to the chapel.

In the spandrels of the three-light windows there are eighteen *Busts of Saints* set in extremely pointed trilobate aedicules, alternated with the coat of arms of the cardinal patron.

The figure of Cardinal Gentile di Partino da Montefiore appears twice: on the inner facade, kneeling before St. Martin, and in the lower part of the central two-light opening.

The cardinal is buried in the chapel of St. Louis.

On these pages, various episodes in the Life of St. Martin, part of the fresco cycle: the Death of the Saint and the Saint divides his mantle with the poor man.

On the following pages: the episode of St. Martin being knighted by the Emperor Costanzo, and a detail of the same scene, frescoed by Simone Martini in the Chapel of St. Martino.

THE ST. FRANCIS MASTER

The dimensions of the Lower Church are as follows: maximum length, 70.70 m; maximum width, 11.80 m; width of the atrium, 38.80 m; depth of the entrance atrium, 11.20 m; length of every bay, 11.20 m; diameter of the apse, 11.80 m; width of the transept (chapels excluded), 29.40 m; depth of the transept, 12.70 m; height, 10.20 m.

There is a series of frescoes on the walls of the nave which depicts the *Passion of Christ* on the right (*Preparation of the Cross, Crucifixion, Deposition, The Women at the Sepulcher*, and perhaps *The Supper at Emmaus*), and on the left the *Life of St. Francis* (*Consigning his Clothing to his Father*, the *Dream of Innocent III, Sermon to the Birds, St. Francis Receiving the Stigmata, Death of the Saint*). This is the oldest iconographic cycle showing the parallel-

Sermon to the Birds painted by the «St. Francis Master» in the nave of the Lower Church.

Facing page: the tomb of St. Francis.

ism between the life of St. Francis and that of Christ and the oldest pictorial decoration in the Basilica (ca. 1260). It is assigned to an unknown painter called the St. Francis Master, perhaps a pupil of Giunta Pisano.

The artist frescoed the entire wall. But today only fragments of many of the scenes remain, for most of them were destroyed in 1300 when the entrance arches to the side chapels were opened up in the wall of the nave. Particularly hauting in its delicacy and simplicity is the *Sermon to the Birds*.

TOMB OF ST. FRANCIS

The body of St. Francis was placed under the high altar of the Lower Church on May 25, 1230, after it had been kept in the Chapel of St. George for four years immediately after his death. For more than two centuries it could be seen from close up by entering the tomb through a tunnel which led from the choir to the sepulchral chamber. In 1442 the Perugini with Niccolò Piccinino at their head laid waste to the city of Assisi and unsuccessfully attempted to carry off the body of the Saint. They decided to try diplomacy where force had failed and endeavored to convince the pope that the body would be safer in Perugia. But Pope Eugene IV held firm and immediately ordered the entrance tunnel to the tomb to be closed. It was not, however, definitive for in 1449 Niccolò V, successor to Eugene IV, was able to visit the tomb. The last pope to go down was Pope Sixtus IV who then ordered the entrance to be completely closed in 1476.

Various attempts were made to open a breach in the centuries that followed. But none succeeded until 1818. On orders of Pope Pius VII, careful excavation work was begun on October 12th and continued until December 2, 1818 – a total of fifty-two nights. The stone sarcophagus was found, surrounded by an iron grate, set into the living rock and protected by layers of concrete. The mortal remains of the Saint, in the presence of a commission that

consisted of the bishops of Umbria, lay experts, and public notaries, were found in skeletal condition but generally well preserved. It was December 12, 1818. Pope Pius VII, after having acknowledged the entire enterprise in a second document on September 5, 1820, declared «the identity of the body of St. Francis found under the high altar of the Lower Church of Assisi to be certain» and ordered that «the venerable body not be taken elsewhere from the subterranean place in which it had been for almost six centuries... and that the entire sepulcher be beautified... and that a more suitable entrance be opened».

Work began in 1822 on a project by Pasquale Belli, terminating in 1824. The result was a crypt in neoclassic style which not many approved of. After various studies, between 1926 and 1932 the architect Ugo Tarchi built the simple and austere installation that we see now.

At present then the basilica complex consists of three levels.

On January 24, 1978, on the orders of Pope Paul VI, a re-examination was effected which confirmed the precedent data and provided for an improved method of preserving the body of St. Francis. It is at present in a small plexiglass casket, enclosed in the precedent metal casket of 1820, placed in the original stone coffin in which the body was laid in the 13th century. This is what we now see behind the altar.

Four of his first companions are buried around the tomb

of the Saint: Masseo, Angelo, Rufino, Leone.

Right across the way, on the landing where the two flights of stairs that lead to the tomb cross, is the urn with the mortal remains of «Frate Jacopa» dei Settesoli, placed there in 1932.

The votive lamp of the communes of Italy burns in front of the tomb. The oil is offered annually by one of the Italian regions.

Life of St. Francis

Francis, son of Pietro di Bernardone, a wealthy cloth merchant, and of Madonna Pica, was born in Assisi in 1182.

As a youth he led a gay and carefree life, and soon became «king of the revels» in the city. But before long he began to be aware that God had other plans for him. It was not easy for Francis to surrender to the grace of God. His decision matured after he had embraced the leper and became definitive when he heard the Word of God, as it was to be found in the Gospels.

It was the beginning of a long journey of search and expectation which led him to achieve a unique human and spiritual experience, the result of radical coherent choices.

He was a charismatic leader the likes of which will never be found again in history. On the other hand Francis never intended to be a «model», but simply requested others to live the faith that springs from the Gospels, to open themselves to the mystery of God and of man, to be aware of the continuous presence of God in history.

When he died in 1226 he was only forty-four years old and his followers scattered throughout the world numbered in the thousands.

Facing page: the tomb of St. Francis as it is now; below: the mortal remains of the Saint; on the right the stone casket which contains them.

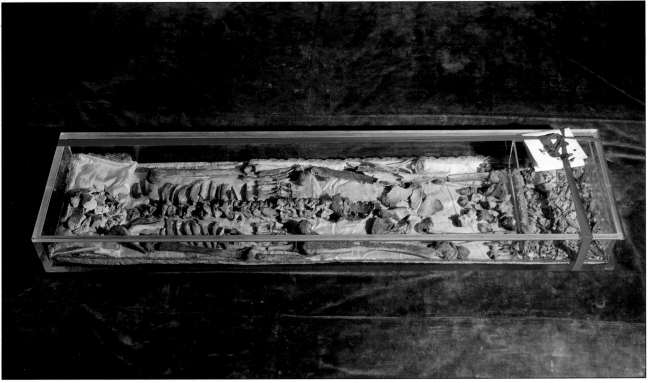

UPPER CHURCH

CLOISTER OF SIXTUS IV

Breathing the air of the Renaissance, this cloister was the result of the patronage of the Franciscan pope, Sixtus IV, who had it built between 1474 and 1476, entrusting Antonio da Como with the task. It is built on two superposed loggias (the capitals are attributed to Francesco Zampa) and is ornamented in the center by a cistern which serves to collect the rain water both from the Basilica and the greater part of the Monastery.

Wandering around the cloister, both above and below, one can note the flying buttresses, the wrought ironwork by local 16th-century craftsmen, and on the walls numerous frescoes by the Assisian painter Dono Doni (ca. 1570), at present unfortunately mostly ruined. They depict scenes from the *Life of St. Francis* and some references to the Saint in the footsteps of Christ.

A spectacular view of the apse of the Basilica is to be had from the shadows of the cloister. High and luminous, it

Two views of the enchanting Cloister of Sixtus IV.

looms up, semicircular below and polygonal at the top, lightened above by Gothic windows, and flanked by two cylindrical pylons.

There are three other cloisters inside the complex of the Sacro Convento, but that of Sixtus IV is the largest and is in a sense the «heart» of the inhabited sector. In the lower part there are various rooms used for cultural activities. In the center is the **Library** with over 80,000 volumes. The most important collections are the over a thousand manuscripts, the 356 incunabuli, the 3500 *cinquecentine* and the 5000 manuscripts, with extremely rare old editions. In the 14th and 15th centuries it was one of the most important libraries in Europe, surpassed only by that of the Sorbonne in Paris and that of the pope in Avignon. It currently centers its attention on the specifically Franciscan aspects, theology, music, art history.

The «Museum-Treasury» of the Basilica is in the upper part of the cloister and houses many objects of church art, vestments and tapestries, paintings of various centuries. In the innermost part is the **Sala Alitalia** with the **Perkins Collection**, the most important collection of Italian medieval to Renaissance art in Assisi. The American art critic Frederick Mason Perkins (1874-1955) bequeathed it as a permanent donation to the Sacro Convento of San Francesco. The fifty-seven pieces, mostly panel paintings, are of Sienese, Florentine, Venetian, Veronese and Emilian school, by artists active in the 14th-16th centuries. These include: Pietro Lorenzetti, Taddeo di Bartolo, Masolino da Panicale, Lorenzo Monaco, Sassetta, Pier Francesco Fiorentino, Signorelli, Fra Angelico and others.

FACADE OF THE UPPER CHURCH

The simple but harmonious façade of the Upper Basilica, with, to the right, some details.

On the following pages: a marvelous overall view of the interior of the Upper Basilica.

The exterior of the Upper Church is extremely simple, undecorated and with a minimum of architectural elements almost as if it were underscoring the idea of Franciscan simplicity and served simply as an entrance for the artistic and spiritual wealth to be found inside.

In its basic lines and in the rose window that elegantly dominates the central register, the facade is Romanesque. It is purely Gothic in the fine twin portals in French style. The result is a strikingly beautiful architectural whole, severe and well balanced, in the pink and white stone of Mt. Subasio. The facade is divided into three parts.

The **lower level** is characterized by the Gothic double portal, facing east, over which is set a pointed arch with a blind rose window in the spandrel.

The **intermediate level** is rectangular in form and separated from the lower level by a rich frieze of floral and animal motifs, with two symbolic eagles at either end. At the center is an exquisite rose window in Cosmati work composed of 116 colonnettes, once faced with mosaic. It is supported by the symbols of the Evangelists: the man/angel for St. Matthew, the ox for St. Luke, the lion for St. Mark and the eagle for St. John.

The **upper level** is triangular in the form of a tall gable with a small oculus at the center.

A wing with an upper loggia, known as the «Benediction Loggia», is attached to the left side of the facade. It was constructed by Valentino Martelli in 1607 and terminates in a tower topped by a hemispherical dome.

The visitor remains breathless upon crossing the threshold of this privileged place, the shining goal for men who are pervaded by the «melancholy yearning of not being saints» and which has been aptly defined by Venturi as «the most beautiful house of prayer» and by Schlosser as the «typical example of Italian Gothic».

The single aisle of the interior is divided into bays and rises high, luminous and light. Slender elegant clusters of columns are set against the walls from which pointed arches and ribbed vaults spring. A vague idea is furnished by the measurements: length, 76 m; width, 13.50 m; width of the transept, 30.10 m; maximum width of the apse, 12.80 m; length of the first bay, 13.30 m; length of the second and third bays, 12.30 m; height, 18 m.

Light enters from the two ample two-light openings with their magnificent stained glass as well as through the rose window, and provides a sense of joy and serenity.

THE CYCLE OF GIOTTO'S FRESCOES

Giotto di Bondone was born in Colle di Vespignano in the valley of the Mugello in 1267 and died in Florence in 1337. His early training was with Cimabue in Florence, from 1280 to 1290, and his talents soon came to the fore, making him one of the great geniuses in the field of painting. His major works are in Assisi, Padua and Florence, although many other cities were distinguished by his presence and still today have some of his masterpieces.

His first experience in Assisi dates to between 1290 and 1295 when he was barely twenty-five and frescoed some of the biblical episodes in the upper part of the Upper Church. Of particular intensity is the scene with *Isaac and Esau*, but also the fresco with the four doctors of the Latin church, *Gregory, Augustine, Ambrose*, and *Jerome*.

His continuous visits to Rome and his encounter with the classic painting and the Roman school of Cavallini soon matured his personality and set him on the road to full artistic maturity.

It was at this time that the Minister-General Fra Giovanni di Muro entrusted him with the task of frescoing the Upper Church with the *Life of the holy «Poverello»*. Giotto executed the work between 1297 and 1299, realizing the marvelous cycle of frescoes of the «Legend of St. Francis». He left the schemes of Byzantine Romanesque art behind and adopted others that were less severe and more human, more lifelike and more violent. One of his contemporaries, Cennini, expressed it as follows: «Giotto translated the art of painting from Greek to Latin, and made it modern; his art was the most accomplished that anyone ever had».

The Franciscan theme was not new in art. The cycle by the so-called St. Francis Master already existed in the Lower Church of Assisi. But Giotto succeeded in being truly independent and imposed his own personality and his own creative originality.

From the very beginning frescoes had been planned for in the Upper Church and they are an integral part of the architecture in a spatial, luminous, almost aerial dimension.

The events in the *Life of St. Francis* are set on the lower part of the nave and the inner facade, on either side of the entrance wall. The twenty-eight scenes are divided into groups of three per bay, except for the first bay from the entrance in which there are four. In addition there is a fresco to the right and one to the left of the entrance door. The cycle begins on the right of the altar, with one's back to the entrance.

Giotto was not alone in painting these frescoes but was amply aided by disciples and some older painters, especially of the Roman school. The work moreover was done in haste (Giotto was continuously being pressed with requests from Rome and Florence) and remained unfinished as far as Giotto's hand is concerned, especially in the last scenes. This is why the cycle, marvelous and unified as it may be, is wanting here and there and a number of art critics have raised doubts as to the paternity of Giotto for some of the frescoes.

From the point of view of religion, Giotto was inspired by the «Legenda Major» of St. Bonaventura and quotations from his writings were set under the frescoes. At present these Latin inscriptions are practically illegible. In the following pages, under each picture, the original captions are given in line with a faithful reconstruction by Father Bonaventura Marinangeli.

Bonaventura's vision of faith and his interpretation of the life of the Poverello are evident in their triple aspect of love for God, for man and for His creatures. The frescoes have adopted this threefold theme as their basis and they are presented, in a medieval key, in a perfect mutual relationship. The picture of Francis which emerges is that of a decisive, vigorous person, simple in appearance and in dress, a lover of creation and God's creatures, sharing the sufferings of man, receptive to God and His presence in the vicissitudes of man.

As far as art is concerned, Giotto succeeded in making a break with the precedent Byzantine and Gothic painting, opening the way for his own original contribution in the three-dimensionality of the image, the inclusion of landscape, the attention to surrounding reality, a simple and imposing architectural structure, the rediscovery of the individual and the way in which the figures become living beings, a style full of human significance bound to the present.

A dialogue with St. Francis can be initiated by any visitor who approaches Giotto's frescoes, where he can easily follow the stages in the life of the Saint and perceive the richness of its message.

When Giotto left Assisi, his efficient and highly organized workshop, composed of a host of followers, remained behind. They continued to fresco many parts, particularly in the Lower Church, perhaps in part under the attentive eye of the master. In Assisi, Giotto's hand can be identified without the shadow of a doubt in the chapel dedicated to the Magdalen in the Lower Church. It is a mature Giotto who returned to Assisi after having frescoed the Scrovegni Chapel in Padua. This is evident in the *Noli me Tangere*, in the great puissance of the figure and in the perfection of the landscape. The details in the *Resurrection of Lazarus* are perfect.

Giotto's work is to be found in many Italian cities, especially Rome, Padua, Rimini, Florence. But Assisi will always be an essential stage for an understanding of this great Florentine master. Even though he was to return once more to the Franciscan theme in the Basilica of Santa Croce in Florence, the marvelous synthesis of painting-architecture-theology Giotto achieved in Assisi was unique.

In recent years scholars have attempted to relate the twenty-eight frescoes of the Legend of St. Francis to the thirty-four frescoes in the upper zone of the nave of the Upper Church (with sixteen *Scenes from the Old Testament* and eighteen from the *New Testament*), recreating a closer parallelism between the «story of salvation» and the «life of St. Francis». The result is a marvelous catechesis. The figure of St. Francis appears fully illustrated both in the sense of the Old and of the New Testment.

Without the shadow of a doubt it can be affirmed that Giotto has glorified St. Francis... but also that St. Francis has glorified Giotto!

St. Vittorino, St. Rufino, St. Francis and St. Clare, frescoed by Giotto underneath the arch on the counter-façade, framed by elegant architectural decorations (lost).

The vault, splendidly frescoed by Giotto, with portraits of the Four Doctors of the Church: St. Gregory, St. Augustine, St. Ambrose and St. Jerome (partially lost).

The twenty-eight episodes from the Life of St. Francis

1. *Francis honored by a simple man.*

«An ordinary citizen of Assisi spreads his cloak on the ground before the Blessed Francis and gives honor to his passage, in addition asserting, inspired one may believe by God, that Francis was worthy of respect and reverence, because he was soon going to accomplish great things, and therefore was to be honored by all».

2. *The dream of the palace filled with weapons in Spoleto.*

«The Blessed Francis, having fallen asleep the next night, saw a splendid and sumptuous palace with weapons embellished with the sign of the cross of Christ, and when he asked to whom this belonged, the answer was given from on high that it would all belong to him and his knights».

3. *Francis gives away his cloak to an impoverished knight.*

«The Blessed Francis chanced to meet a noble knight, destitute and poorly dressed and, moved to compassion by his poverty, he immediately took off his cloak and dressed him in it».

4. *Before the Crucifix of San Damiano.*

«The Blessed Francis, praying before an image of the Crucified Saviour, a voice came down from the cross saying: Francis go and repair my house which is falling completely into ruin, meaning by this the Roman Church».

5. *Renouncing all worldly goods.*

«The Blessed Francis gave back everything to his father, and taking off his clothes renounced his paternal goods and lands, saying: Henceforth with all certainty I can say: Our Father who art in heaven, because Pietro di Bernardone has repudiated me».

6. *The dream of Pope Innocent III.*

«The pope saw the Lateran Basilica about to collapse and a small poor man, that is the Blessed Francis, put his shoulders to the building and held it up to keep it from falling».

7. *Oral approval of the Franciscan rule.*

«Pope Innocent III approved the Rule and gave permission to preach conversion, and permitted the friars who had accompanied the Saint to wear the tonsure so they might preach the divine word».

8. *Rivotorto, apparition to the friars on a chariot of fire.*

«The Blessed Francis was praying in a hovel and was bodily far from his friars who were gathered together in the hovel outside the city. They saw the Blessed Francis on a bright chariot of fire, moving around the place close to midnight, while the hovel was illuminated as bright as day, to the amazement of those who were awake and those who were asleep woke up and were frightened».

9. *The place of Francis in paradise.*

«A vision from above showed a friar many thrones in heaven and one which was more glorious than the others, and he heard a voice say to him: This throne belonged to one of the angels who fell for their pride, and it is now reserved for the humble Francis».

10. *The demons cast out of Arezzo.*

«The Blessed Francis saw many exulting demons over the city of Arezzo and said to his follower Silvestro: Go and in the name of God cast out the demons... shouting at the gates; and as he obeyed and shouted, the demons of the division fled and peace was immediately restored to the citizens of Arezzo».

11. *Trial by fire before the Sultan of Egypt.*

«The Blessed Francis, in testimony to the truth of the faith of Christ, challenged the priests of the Sultan of Babylonia to walk into a great fire with him, but none of them was willing to go with him, but all fled immediately from the presence of the Saint and the Sultan».

12. *The ecstasy of Francis.*

«The Blessed Francis, one day while he was in fervent prayer, was seen by the friars raised above the ground with his whole body, his arms extended heavenward: and a bright cloud enveloped him».

13. *The crib at Greccio.*

«The Blessed Francis, in memory of Christmas ordered straw to be fetched, and that an ox and an ass be brought; then he gave a sermon on the birth of the poor King; and while the holy man was in prayer, a knight saw the Infant Jesus in place of the one the Saint had placed there».

Following pages:

14. *A spring of fresh water for the thirsty man.*

«The Blessed Francis, ascending a mountain on the back of a poor man's donkey, since he was ailing, prayed for this man who was dying of thirst and caused water to come forth from a rock, water which had never been there before nor reappeared afterwards».

15. *The sermon to the birds.*

«The Blessed Francis, on his way to Bevagna, preached to many birds, who, fluttering with joy, stretched out their necks, flapped their wings, opened their beaks and touched his tunic; and all this was seen by his followers who were waiting at the roadside».

16. *Prediction of the death of a knight.*

«The Blessed Francis implored the grace of salvation for a knight of Celano, who devotedly had invited him to dinner, and after having made confession and having set his affairs in order, while the others were at table, suddenly he died and fell asleep in the Lord».

17. *Sermon before Honorius III.*

«The Blessed Francis preached so devoutly and so efficaciously before the Pope and the Cardinals that it was clear that he spoke not with learned words of human wisdom but by divine inspiration».

18. *Apparition to the Friars at the Chapter.*

«While the Blessed Anthony of Padua was preaching at the Chapter of Arles about the cross, the Blessed Francis who was not bodily there appeared and, extending his hands, blessed the friars, as was seen by a certain Monaldo; and the other friars rejoiced immensely».

19. *Francis receiving the stigmata.*

«The Blessed Francis, preaching on the slope of the Mount of La Verna, saw Christ in the form of a crucified seraphim which imprinted in his hands and feet and right side the sacred stigmata of our Lord and Saviour Jesus Christ».

20. *Encounter with sister death.*

«In the hour of death of the Blessed Francis, a friar saw his soul ascend to heaven in the form of a brilliant star».

21. *Apparition after his death.*

«At the very moment when the Saint died, Brother Augustine, Minister in southern Italy, sick and near death, and for some time already deprived of speech, cried out and said: Wait for me, Father, I am coming with you; whereupon he died and followed his Holy Father. The bishop of Assisi, moreover, on Monte S. Michael Archangel, saw the Blessed Francis who said to him: See, I am going to heaven».

22. *Proof of the stigmata.*

«When the body of the Blessed Francis was lying at the Porziuncola, Messer Jerome, a famous doctor and scholar, moved the nails, and, with his own hands, examined the hands and feet and ribs of the Saint».

23. *The grief of the Poor Clares.*

«The crowd which had assembled, carrying to Assisi, with branches of trees and a great number of lighted candles, the sacred body, adorned with the celestial gems, showed it to the Blessed Clare and the other virgins consecrated to God».

24. *Canonization of Francis.*

«The Holy Pope came in person to the city of Assisi, diligently examined the miracles, on the basis of the testimony of the friars, canonized the Blessed Francis and enrolled him in the calendar of the saints».

25. *Reassurance as to the truth of the stigmata.*

«When Pope Gregory rather doubted of the wound in his side, the Blessed Francis told him in a dream: Give me an empty vial; and when he received it, he was seen filling it with blood from his side».

26. *Curing a sick man.*

«The Blessed Francis, undoing with his hands the bandages and delicately touching the wounds, immediately and perfectly cured Giovanni di Ilerda who was deathly ill and for whom the doctors had no hope, but who had devoutly prayed to him when he was wounded».

27. *Resurrecton of a woman who had died in sin.*

«The Blessed Francis resuscitated this woman who had died, who then in the presence of the clergy and others confessed a sin she had not yet confessed, died again, she went to sleep in the Lord and the devil fled confused».

28. *Liberation of a prisoner.*

«The Blessed Francis freed this prisoner accused of heresy, and by order of the Pope entrusted to the Bishop; this happened on the feast of the Blessed Francis, on the eve of which the prisoner had fasted according to the custom of the church».

CIMABUE'S FRESCOES

The apse and the transept of the Upper Church were decorated by Cimabue. The colors have changed considerably but it nevertheless remains the highest example of his art. As the Byzantine and early Medieval forms were gradually left behind, the way was paved for Giotto.

Cimabue, Cenno di Pepo, was born in Florence around 1240. As a youth he frequented the friars, both Dominican and Franciscan, and began to paint for them in Arezzo, in Pisa and in Florence. He was called to Rome by Pope Gregory IX and thanks to the friendship of Cardinal Gaetano Orsini, entered into close relations with the Roman school of Jacopo Torriti, Pietro Cavallini and Filippo Rusuti. He accompanied them to Assisi in the spring of 1278 and while Torriti, Rusuti and Cavallini frescoed the nave with *Scenes from the Old and New Testaments*, Cimabue terminated the frescoes of the entire apse area by the end of 1285. Back in Florence, he died around 1300.

The right arm of the transept is frescoed with *Scenes from the Acts of the Apostles* concerning Saints Peter and Paul; a *Crucifixion* and (above) the *Transfiguration* and *Christ in Glory*.

In the apse, scenes from the *Life of the Madonna*.

On the vault of the sanctuary, the *Four Evangelists* with

The large scene of the Crucifixion in the Upper Church; St. Francis kneels at the foot of the Cross.

the cities they evangelized: St. Matthew in Jerusalem, St. Mark in Rome, St. Luke in Corinth, and St. John in Ephesus.

In the left arm of the transept, scenes from the Apocalypse and, behind the altar, the large scene of the *Crucifixion*.

Cimabue painted as if he were painting on panel, with tempera, and the intonaco on the wall was not well prepared so that humidity seeped through and altered the colors. Moreover he used the poisonous white lead in mixing his colors which blackened with time. This transformation of the light areas into dark ones makes the entire fresco look like an enormous photographic negative.

Even so the imposing scene of the *Crucifixion* remains highly dramatic. Above, the weeping angels fly around the crucified figure, receiving His blood in a chalice; below, two groups of figures express opposing feelings – some in favor, some against, Christ; at the foot of the cross, St. Francis.

CHOIR STALLS OF THE UPPER CHURCH

Below Cimabue's frescoes stand the lovely imposing wooden choir stalls, like a great monument which fits perfectly into the art of the Upper Church. Commissioned in 1491 by the Minister General of the Order, Francesco Sansone, they were finished in 1501 after ten years of work by Domenico Indovini from San Severino Marche, and a host of master carvers. At the time the entire work cost 755 gold ducats.

Finely carved and inlaid, the 102 stalls are in Venetian-Gothic Style – a late pre-Renaissance Gothic. Each stall has a gabled frontispiece with a rich rose carved in the center and slender pinnacles on either side.

Under the gable each stall has an aedicule, sixty-eight of them, with a shell-shaped niche. They are of classical inspiration and are painted in blue and gold. On the back panels of the stalls is a beautiful series of portraits of saints, scholars, writers, dignitaries of the Franciscan Order. The entire gallery is a hymn to the Franciscan faith. Each panel is enclosed in an intarsia frame and each figure is set under a halo-like arch. The lively half-length figures are seen from the front or from the side, and are depicted with considerable psychological subtleties. Two of the figures are particularly striking: the *Madonna* and the *Archangel Gabriel* (on the outer corner where the choir stalls turn into the apse). The tender delicate figures turn towards each other and together they form an *Annunciation*. Below these stalls with aedicules is a second tier of stalls, thirty-four in number, with a wealth of carving and inlays, with architectural perspectives and stylized foliage. The perspectives in the panels set at the head of the transept are particularly lovely.

The choir stalls are separated at the back center of the apse by the *papal throne* of 1250, composed of disparate elements from various sources.

A *lectern* just as fine as the choir stalls is set in front of the throne. It consists of two parts: a base and the lectern itself, which turns on its axis. The base is highly decorated with intarsias of floral compositions and the figures of St. Francis and St. Anthony on the side panels. The lectern has tarsias of two open «*Kiriali*» with the Gregorian notes of the *Kyrie* and of the *Gloria* of the «*Cum jubilo*» mass.

The Archangel Gabriel and the Madonna, the two wood intarsias in the choir stalls of the Upper Church which seen together depict the Annunciation.

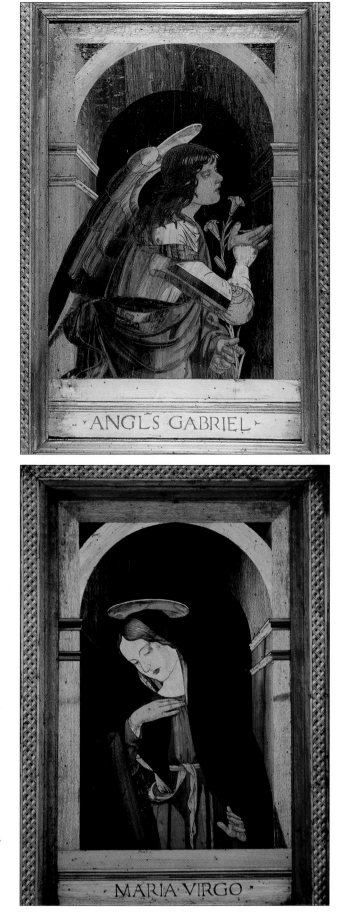

STAINED-GLASS WINDOWS

The basilicas were most magical when the light was filtered by the stained-glass windows made by German, French, Italian masters. Even though they are not integrally preserved, the twenty-eight original windows constitute the «summa vitraria» of the 13th and 14th centuries. The collection has three firsts as far as beauty and historical importance are concerned: it is the oldest in Italy; the cartoons were made by the greatest masters of the time (Cimabue, Giotto, Simone Martini); it is the most complete ensemble in the variety of styles and techniques used.

The individual windows irradiate and transmit the natural light to the interior which is transformed by the marvelous play of colors.

The first to be made around the middle of the 13th century were the stained-glass windows in the apse of the Upper Church. Next came those of the nave. Those in the Lower Church date to the early 14th century onwards. The subjects are either biblical (*Old* and *New Testament themes*) or figures of *Saints*.

The stained-glass windows of the Basilicas are superb, as illustrated by the detail of that with Jesus Christ and St. Francis (left), and by the overall view of the stained-glass window in the south transept of the Upper Basilica.

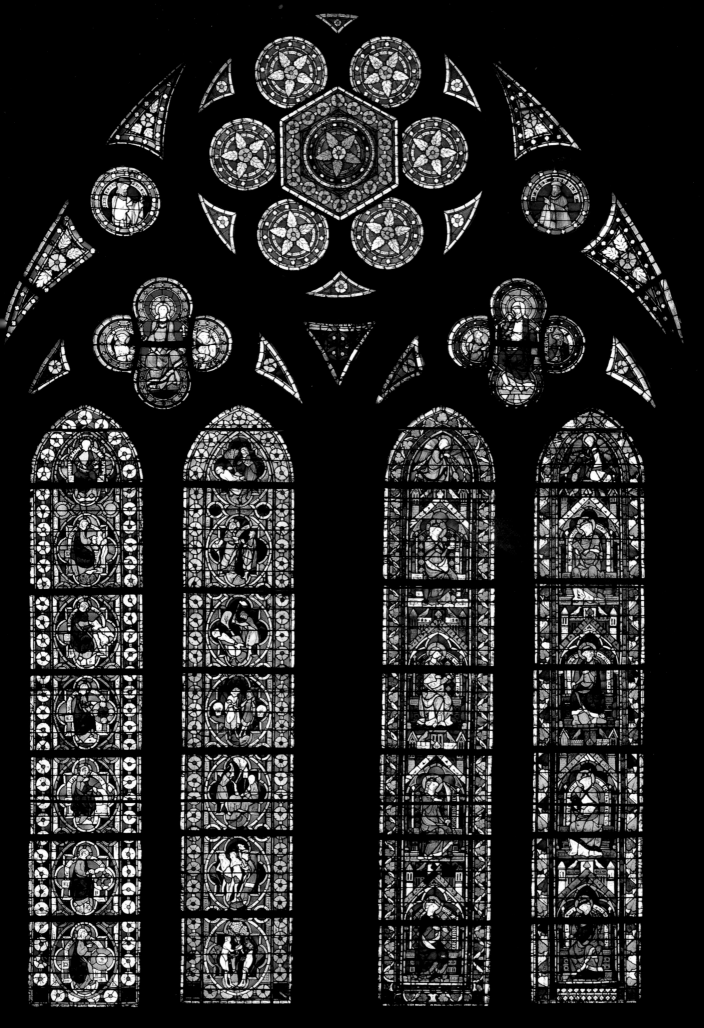

Some marvelous details of the luminous stained-glass windows depicting the main episodes in the life of Christ. Centre: an overall view of the apse of the Upper Basilica, adorned by an authentic lacework of colors.

THE TOWN OF ASSISI

Architects, masons, stone carvers have given Assisi its unique aspect. Time seems to have come to a standstill. The Middle Ages reign sovereign. The pattern of the streets is that of a medieval town clinging to the slopes of a mountain. The principal thoroughfares move horizontally along the mountain rising towards the Piazza del Comune. They are joined to each other at right angles by steep streets, lanes, with arches, ramps, and stairs.

The streets are lined by medieval houses, all built with the stone of Mt. Subasio which comes alive after a rain, red in the warm light of sunset, pale in the light of the moon or when it reflects the snow. The doorways, often with Gothic arches, are also in stone. The principal entrance with its threshold right on a level with the street is almost always

Some charming images of the picturesque streets of Assisi, overlooked by ancient stone houses. Narrow steps and distinctive fountains recreate a medieval atmosphere.

flanked by a second walled-up entrance that is narrower and has a much higher threshold. This is the «door of the dead» which was opened only to let the coffin pass and was then immediately closed.

The windows with their circlets of wrought iron are filled with flowers which gladden the streets and delight the soul of the visitor.

The **city walls**, a symbol and guarantee of safety, enclose the entire city center. The walls themselves could tell many tales for they were initially built by the Umbri and then the Romans before being destroyed in the Barbarian invasion. Rebuilt from scratch in 1198-1199, they were enlarged in 1300 to their present form to include the basilicas of San Francesco and Santa Chiara and the abbey of San Pietro.

The perimeter of the walls is about five kilometers.

The eight entrances to the city help the visitor feel that he is really living in times past and complete the picture of the urban layout of the city. Three of the gates date to the 12th century (**Porta San Giacomo, Porta Perlici, Porta Moiano**) and three to the 14th century (**Porta San Francesco, Porta Nuova, Porta San Pietro**).

MONTE FRUMENTARIO, MUSEUM OF THE ROMAN FORUM AND THE TEMPLE OF MINERVA

Umbria was first invaded by the Romans under the Consul Quinto Fabio in 309 B.C. This was when Assisi entered the Roman orbit, eventually becoming a *municipium romanum* which meant that it had to have a forum, a temple, baths, a theater, and an amphitheater.

Traces of these structures still exist in Assisi. The **Temple of Minerva** is in the Piazza del Comune and under the square are the remains of the **forum**; not far from the center, at the outskirts near the city walls, are traces of the **baths**; what remains of the **theater** is next to the cathedral of San Rufino; the remains of the **amphitheater** are near Porta Perlici. In addition various archaeological finds are scattered throughout the city center.

Climbing from the Basilica of San Francesco towards the Piazza del Comune, the visitor encounters the **Monte Frumentario** at the beginning of the Via San Francesco and the **Museum of the Roman Forum** at the beginning of the Via Portica.

The Monte Frumentario is a structure dating back to 1267. It was originally a hospice for the poor, and then became the seat of an Istituto di Credito Agrario (bank) and is now used for cultural exhibitions. The portico is particularly lovely, with its charming Byzantine and Romanesque-Gothic arches and capitals.

The Roman Museum houses Etruscan urns and stone cippi as well as inscriptions, epigraphs, capitals from the Roman period. Two mutilated Roman statues and a sarcophagus of the 2nd century A.D. are rather interesting.

Originally the Roman forum was four meters lower than the present square. During the excavations of 1938 the old Roman pavement and a long wall that served as base for the Temple of Minerva above were found. In front of the wall there is a rectangular base elevated on two steps (perhaps the Tribunal); another base at the center of the Forum was for a monument which an inscription identifies as the statues of the Dioscuri, Castor and Pollux. The Piazza del Comune lies a few steps from the Museum of the Roman Forum, with the marvelously preserved temple dedicated to Minerva. Originally the ground level was lower and two steps led up to the temple which, being higher, was more aerial and elegant. Even so its external beauty is still intact. It is a Corinthian hexastyle temple, dating to the early Empire. The pronoas has six fluted columns with support the trabeation and the low pediment. It is distinguished by a purity of line, harmonious proportions, an exquisite elegance, and with a particularly lovely tonality of stone.

Above: the elegant portico of the Monte Frumentario; facing page: a view of the Piazza del Comune with the Palazzo del Capitano del Popolo, the Torre del Comune and the Temple of Minerva.

The excellently preserved façade of the Temple of Minerva, flanked by the mighty Torre del Comune.

Long and narrow, the Piazza del Comune as it is now occupies approximately the site of the old Roman forum and holds the same role as center for civic life. The square is important because of the monuments on all sides.
About the Temple of Minerva, in his *Italian Journey*, Goethe wrote: «... here it is, before my eyes, that illustrious monument... A relatively small temple, suited to a small town and, nevertheless, so perfect, so well thought out, that it would be striking anywhere... I could not get my fill of contemplating the facade, in such a genial logical way had the artist dealt with it... Words are not enough to express all that the contemplation of this monument aroused in me; its fruits will be eternal».

In 1539, with the concession of Paul III, the building was consecrated as a church and dedicated to the Virgin as «Santa Maria sopra Minerva».
The interior was modified in 1634 by Giorgetti and then in the 18th century by F. Appiani.

PALAZZO DEL CAPITANO DEL POPOLO AND THE PALAZZO DEI PRIORI

The **Torre del Comune** (or del Popolo), forty-five meters high, rises near the temple. It is square and crowned by Ghibelline crenellation. Begun in 1275, it was finished in 1305. At the top of the tower is the «Campana delle Laudi», (bell of praise) which weighs 4000 kilograms and was offered by the Communes of Italy in 1926. At its base is a sampling of the measures once valid in Assisi, incised into bricks and tiles.

Next to the tower is the **Palazzo del Capitano del Popolo** or of the Podestà, dating to 1282. It consists of three floors with Guelph crenellations at the top.

The **Palazzo dei Priori**, seat of the town hall, is on the other side of the square. Erected in 1337 and restored in 1927, it is formed of three sections built in different times. One of the rooms is known as the «Room of the Conciliation» because in 1926 it was used to lay the foundations for the dialogue which led to the signing of the Lateran Pact between the Italian state and the Papal state.

The lower part of the building houses the **Pinacoteca Comunale** (picture gallery) with about a hundred works by various painters from the 14th century on.

The 18th century fountain in Piazza del Comune, and two pictures of the powerful tower, with its crenellated top, which rises above it.

CALENDIMAGGIO

The Calendimaggio (beginning, *calende*, of May) is a festival for the beginning of spring and can be related to the customs of various peoples to celebrate the rites of spring. The first Calendimaggio in Assisi was promoted by Arnaldo Fortini in 1927. In its present form it dates to 1954. The city, divided into the «parte de sopra» (upper part) and the «parte de sotto» (lower part), in keeping with a rivalry that dates back to the 14th century, becomes alive for three days with all kinds of exhibitions in a marvelous playing of parts.

It all begins with flags and banners flown throughout the city, the announcement of the festival by the crier and the opening of the taverns. The first afternoon, after a short procession, the standards are blessed: those of the «parte de sotto» at San Francesco and those of the «parte de so-pra» at San Rufino. In the Piazza del Comune the «Maestro di Campo» assumes the sovereign powers of the city for the duration of the festivities. In the evening, re-evocations of medieval life in the quarters of the «parte de sotto».

On the second day there are medieval contests in the Piazza del Comune and the exhibition of the cross-bow archers for the proclamation of the Madonna Primavera. In the evening, re-evocations of medieval life in the quarters of the «parte de sopra».

On the third day, in the afternoon, the historical procession of both parts and the reading of the proclamations of challenge. In the evening, with torches illuminating the streets, there is a singing contest between the two parts and the assigning of the Palio or trophy.

The beauty of the costumes, the vivacity of the crowds, the striving for victory, the well-reconstructed medieval atmosphere provide the visitor with a truly unique experience.

FOUNTAINS

The fountain is a monument to water and a sign of life for the human community. Water reawakens the joy of living and provides the opportunity for human encounters.

A number of fountains beautify the urban layout in Assisi. Two of them, together with any number of historical recollections, can also be considered small works of art.

In the Via San Francesco, next to the Monte Frumentario, is the **Fonte Oliviera**, built in 1570 by Oliviero Federici. Over the spouts is the warning: «a fine of one scudo and the loss of the clothes for whoever washes in this fountain».

In the Via Fontebella, the **Fonte Marcella** is named after the Sienese Marcello Tuto who had it built in 1556. It consists of a rectangular basin, subdivided into panels with coats of arms, flowers and leaves. The water comes out of three masks.

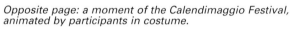

Opposite page: a moment of the Calendimaggio Festival, animated by participants in costume.

Two details of the 16th century Fonte Marcella.

THE BLESSED TOWN

Shortly before his death, as St. Francis was on his way to Santa Maria degli Angeli from Assisi, he stopped halfway down. Turning towards his city he blessed her with these words: «May you be blessed by God, holy city, for through you many souls will be saved and many servants of God will dwell in you and many of yours will be elected to the realm of eternal life».

The Saint's benediction came true and in all centuries the city has been a «spiritual city», a «new Jerusalem». Innumerable elect souls have paused here or have come to Assisi for religious reasons alone.

Those who climb this holy mount realize that the spirit of St. Francis is still alive and that the values of Franciscan spirituality (a culture of love, a civilization of peace, search for God, love of nature, gift of work, universal brotherhood, eucumenical obedience to the holy mother church) are within the reach of all. St. Francis is the never-ending gift of God to the church and to the world.

The worldwide day of prayer for peace which took place in Assisi on October 27, 1986 has induced many to divide the history of religion in our times into «before Assisi and after Assisi». Visiting the cathedral of San Rufino, the basilica of Santa Chiara and all the other small and large sanctuaries in the city, one becomes aware that the words «prayer», «peace», «brotherhood» are not empty words, but values which complete the life of man. It is what is commonly called «the spirit of Assisi».

The town, its craft shops, its fountains and its houses.

CATHEDRAL OF SAN RUFINO

The cathedral of Assisi is dedicated to the martyr St. Rufino. The present church was preceded by a «*parvula basilica*» erected in the 8th century to receive and house the mortal remains of the saint which had been transferred there from the site of his martyrdom on the river Chiascio near Costano in 238.

Around 1028 , after a miraculous event, Bishop Ugone had the preceding church destroyed and erected a new one to which he transferred the episcopal see from Santa Maria Maggiore a few years later in 1035. This church too was soon torn down for in 1134 Bishop Clarissimo had a more solemn and imposing structure built on the site. It

was commissioned from Giovanni da Gubbio by the archpriest Ranieri and the campanile was also raised a story.

The work begun in 1140 went ahead slowly. It was not until 1253 that Pope Innocent IV officially consecrated the holy building. But services were already being held in the church at the altar which had been consecrated in 1228 by Pope Gregory IX when he was in Assisi for the canonization of St. Francis.

The **facade** clearly testifies to this discontinuity in the building, with its three superposed registers: the lower

The austere Cathedral of St. Rufino with, to the right, a detail of the elaborate central rose window.

zone dates to the 12th century, while the top is a hundred years later, conceived and built in forms that are already extraneous to the Romanesque style.

The *lower zone* is characterized by a surface divided into panels which increase in height from bottom to top and lead the eye upwards. Three portals, richly decorated with various geometric designs and animals, are set into the facade. The lunette of the central portal contains the figure of *Christ enthroned* with the Madonna nursing Jesus on the left and St. Rufino on the right. At the base of the central portal are two lions and at the base of the side portals are griffins. The lunette of the left portal depicts two lions drinking from a vase, while that on the right has two birds.

The *middle zone* begins with a gallery of small arches with columns and capitals in classical style. The gallery is supported by brackets decorated with a great variety of heads of men and animals. Three rose windows set into the center of the middle zone let light into the church as well as being ornamental elements. The four *symbols of the evangelists* are set around the central rose window which is supported by three human beings resting on animals.

The *upper zone* is undecorated except for a large blind ogee arch inscribed in the triangular gable.

On account of its instability, the **interior** of the cathedral was radically remodelled by Galeazzo Alessi after 1567. It has a nave and two aisles, divided by massive piers. Worthy of mention in the interior, in addition to some fine 17th and 18th century canvases, especially those by Dono Doni, are the *baptismal font*, to be found at the entrance of the right aisle, where St. Francis, St. Clare, Frederick II of Swabia and almost all of Francis' first companions were baptized; the *oratory of St. Francis* where the Saint withdrew to pray before preaching in the cathedral. It can be reached from the sacristy; on either side of the high altar the statues of *St. Francis* and *St. Clare* by Giovanni Dupré (1881) and behind the altar, the figure of *St. Rufino* by Padre Lemoyne (1823). The *Roman cistern* (1st cent. A.D.), on which the bell tower is built is at the entrance to the left aisle.

Left: one of the lions flanking the central portal of St. Rufino. Above, the baptismal font and a detail of the Roman sarcophagus which holds the remains of St. Rufino in the cathedral's crypt.

On the following pages: the front of the 14th-century Standard of the Fraternity of St. Rufino, with St. Francis between angels and orderlies; facing page: the back of the Standard with the Crucifixion, the Stigmata of St. Francis and St. Leonard.

Remains of Ugone's original basilica are to be found in the «crypt» and in the cloister next to the square.
The *crypt* lies under the cathedral and has three aisles with cross vaulting and an apse. It contains a *sarcophagus* from the Roman period (3rd cent.) in which the body of St. Rufino was laid.

CHAPTER MUSEUM

Next to the cathedral is the Chapter Museum which contains church vestments, fragments of columns, Roman inscriptions and various canvases of the Umbrian school, including a fine triptych by Nicolo Alunno and one by the Assisan Puccio Capanna.
Particular note should be paid to the *Standard of the Fraternity of St. Rufino* by an unknown late 14th-century Umbrian painter. This gonfalon is painted on both sides – on one is St. Francis enthroned between music-making angels, with the members of the fraternity with a corpse in their midst; on the other side above is the Crucifixion, with the stigmata of St. Francis and St. Leonard below with two orderlies.
It is highly likely that the processional gonfalon came from the confraternity of St. Francis, know as that of St. Leonard or the Stigmata.
The iconography of the stories was inspired by the frescoes in the Lower Church. The reference to the vaults, to Lorenzetti, to Giotto's Crucifix are quite evident.

BASILICA OF SANTA CHIARA

The name «Assisi» immediately evokes the name of its most famous son, St. Francis. But his name is intimately linked to that of another child of Assisi, who was sister and friend to him, St. Clare. They both yearned to follow in the footsteps of Jesus Christ and to live according to the Holy Gospels.

Clare was born in Assisi in 1193. Daughter of Favarone di Offreduccio and Ortolana, both from noble families in Assisi, her childhood was passed between Assisi and Perugia. When she was sixteen or seventeen she encountered Francis and his way of life. She was enthralled and after careful meditation decided to embrace the same way of life. Her family however withheld consent even though the Bishop of Assisi Guido had given her his blessing. On the eve of Palm Sunday in 1211 she secretly abandoned her father's house and went to the chapel of the Porziuncola. After having clothed her in religious vestment, Francis had her accompanied first to the Monastery of San Paolo in Bastia and, a few weeks later, to that of Sant'Angelo in Panzo in the environs of Assisi on the slopes of Mt. Subasio. She then passed definitively to San Damiano. After a few months, Clare's example attracted first her sister Agnes and then many other girls from As-

sisi and surroundings. They lived a poor life, as a community segregated from the world. In 1215, after the Lateran Council had decided not to authorize new Rules of religious life, Clare adopted the Rule of St. Benedict, obtaining in addition the privilege of poverty from Innocent IV. Urged by St. Francis, she agreed to become abbess and in her forty-two years at San Damiano her life brought her closer and closer to sainthood, with an original and strongly feminine spirit. With her prayers she closely followed both Francis and the growth of the Franciscan order. Her life of penitence gradually debilitated her. Various prodigious events marked the life of the saint. In 1240, with the force of her prayer, holding the Eucharist she repulsed the Saracens who were besieging Assisi and were about to enter San Damiano. In 1241 she once more successfully intervened against the troops of Vitale of Aversa. On Christmas night in 1252, Clare, immobilized in her cot in San Damiano, took part, as if she were there, in the services in the Basilica of San Francesco. This prodigious event led to her being proclaimed universal patron saint of television in 1958. She died on August 11,

Above: the Basilica of Santa Chiara; facing page: the 13th-century panel by the «St. Clare Master» with the Saint surrounded by eight scenes of episodes in her life.

SANCTA CLARA

1253 and was canonized by Pope Alexander IV in Anagni on August 15, 1255.

Work on the costruction of a basilica in her honor began in 1257, when the Poor Clares ceded their first monastery and the church of San Damiano to the Chapter of San Rufino in exchange for the church of San Giorgio and its holdings.

Construction progressed rapidly under the direction of Fra Filippo da Campello, for on October 3, 1260 the body of the Saint was taken there and the community of the Poor Clares moved from San Damiano to the new convent.

In terms of art, the Basilica of Santa Chiara is in Gothic style, in imitation of the Upper Church of San Francesco. Outside, the church is characterized by the three flying buttresses of the late 14th century. The square campanile rises skywards to the right of the apse.

The gabled **facade**, in white and pink stone, is divided into three registers by cornices set on stone brackets. A single portal opens in the lower zone, a large rose window in the middle zone and a circular oculus in the gable. The Gothic portal, with a round arch, has a shallow splay with three smooth columns in pink and white stone, and capitals with stiff leaves from which smooth ribs rise to follow the line of the arch with a barely pointed external lintel, supported by two roaring lions in roseate stone.

The **interior** of the basilica in Gothic style with cross vaults has a nave only. The two side chapels were added at the beginning of the 14th century. Initially completely frescoed, the walls are now bare as a result of the removal

Above: the vault of the Basilica with frescoes by the «St. Clare Master»; facing page: the Crucifix which spoke to St. Francis, formerly in San Damiano and now in the Chapel of the Crucifix in the basilica.

of the frescoes in the 17th century. A door to the right of the nave leads to the *Chapel of the Crucifix*: on the left is the Crucifix that spoke to St. Francis in San Damiano; in the interior are various important relics: the breviary and tunic of St. Francis, the shirt embroidered by St. Clare, Clare's tunic and cloak and her hair.

Further on is the entrance to the *Chapel of the Santissimo* with frescoes of Giotto's school, including a *Nativity.* This is where the church of San Giorgio formerly stood, at the time outside the city walls. Here St. Francis learned to read when he was a child and received his first religious instruction. Here his mortal remains rested from 1226 to 1230 and here Pope Gregory IX canonized the Saint in 1228.

St. Clare's body also remained here until the basilica was finished.

Entrance to the *crypt* is from the nave. The body of the saint, found in 1850 in a stone sarcophagus under the high altar, can be seen in a crystal casket. It was at that time that the present crypt was built in imitation Gothic style. A small spiral staircase in the center of the crypt makes it possible to glimpse the loculus in which the mortal remains of the saint were enclosed for six centuries.

The final recognition and preservative treatment of the saint's remains were carried out between November 17, 1986 and April 12, 1987.

At the center of the high altar is a majestic 13th-century *Crucifix* by an unknown master. Various frescoes over the sanctuary are well preserved: the vault sections with figures of *Saints* are commonly attributed to Maso di Stefano, of Giotto's workshop.

In the left transept is a fresco depicting the *Nativity* by an anonymous 14th-century Umbrian painter. Even though the picture is mutilated and fragmentary, it closely resembles a similar fresco in the Basilica of San Francesco.

In the right transept is a fine *panel* by the Master of St. Clare, of the 13th century, with the saint in the center surrounded by eight episodes from her life.

Lastly, on the left of the nave is the chapel of St. Agnes, in which some of the saint's first followers are buried. The decoration and the frescoes are of the 1900s.

Tempera on panel for a tabernacle with doors

The Madonna and the blessing Child are on the central panel. On the left: the *Annunciation*, the *Nativity*, the *Adoration of the Magi*, and the *Taking of Christ*. On the right: the *Flagellation*, the *Crucifixion*, the *Deposition*, and the *Pious Women at the Sepulcher*.

In style, the stories are of Byzantine inspiration. The artist was probably Rainaldo di Rainuccio, painter from Spoleto.

SAN FRANCESCO PICCOLINO

A tradition dating to the 15th century narrates that Madonna Pica, already in labor, was unable to deliver her child. A pilgrim appeared and told her that she could give birth only in a stable. The woman obeyed and this oratory is where it is said St. Francis was born.

It is a rustic square structure. Inside there are traces of 13th and 14th-century frescoes. A 14th-century inscription over the entrance reads: «*Hoc oratorium fuit bovis et asini stabulum in quo natus est Francisci mundi speculum*» (This oratory was the stable of an ox and an ass, where Francis, mirror of the world, was born).

The paternal house of St. Francis was in the neighborhood.

SANTA MARIA MAGGIORE

According to some historians the church of «Santa Maria Maggiore» was built on the foundations of a temple of Janus. In fact this area of the town is known as «Moiano», a name which probably derives from «*mons Jani*» (hill of Janus). Not far off there is also a city gate known as «porta di Moiano». During restoration work in 1895, a rectangular room, divided by four monolithic columns, was found under the church. Even further down were the remains of a Roman dwelling, thought by some to be the house of Propertius.

Santa Maria Maggiore was the cathedral of Assisi up to the 1020s. The building as we see it now was rebuilt between 1212-1218 after a fire.

Outside, the church has a spacious **facade** with a gable. It is in simple blocks of ashlar with two entrance portals and the only ornament is a rose window with eight rays, smooth as the spokes of a wheel. It is one of the oldest

Facing page, above: the Church of Santa Maria Maggiore; below: the Oratory of San Francesco Piccolino. Below: the Church of Santa Maria Maggiore and the area of the town known as Moiano.

examples of rose window in Romanesque architecture and was probably by Giovanni da Gubbio, the first architect of the cathedral of San Rufino.

The 14th-century Romanesque campanile stands behind the apse.

The tripartite **interior** with no transept is bare. Only a few fragments of frescoes, almost all of the late 14th century, remain. Of note a *Nativity* of Umbrian school.

Near the sanctuary a staircase leads to the subterranean building. In the left aisle, set against the entrance wall, is the *sarcophagus* found recently and datable to between the 8th and 9th century, on which is a cross between symbolic vines.

Next to the church is the **Vescovado** or *Bishop's palace* where, in a site that traditionally corresponds to the «Sala della rinuncia» the young Francis took off his clothes before Bishop Guido and renounced his paternal inheritance, and where the Saint later spent a few days as a guest of the bishop before going down to die in the Porziuncola...

This same bishop's palace is where Francis reconciled Bishop Guido with the Podestà of Assisi and composed the verse of the Canticle regarding pardon for the occasion: «Praise be to Thee my Lord for those who grant pardon for love of Thee, And bear infirmity and tribulation, Blessed be those who live in peace, For by Thee most High they shall be crowned».

ABBEY OF SAN PIETRO

Upon entering Porta San Pietro one is confronted by a particularly charming sight: an austere church with an unusual dome and a fine square bell tower in Romanesque style. This is the church of San Pietro with a Benedictine abbey annexed. The origins of this abbey dedicated to the Prince of the Apostles are obscure. Up to the beginning of the 14th century it was set outside the city walls and included in the rest of the city only when the new walls were built. The oldest document dates to 1029. The first enlargement probably terminated in 1253. The vaulting of the nave and the dome with its concentric rows of bricks, architecturally of particular interest, are attributed to this period. The funnel-shaped dome, in Arab-Norman style, rises over the sanctuary which is a about a meter higher than the nave.

The tripartite church was consecrated in 1253 by Innocent IV, resident in Assisi. The last great transformation of the building dates to 1268, at the time of Abbot Rustico and work involved the upper part of the facade, among other things.

There are various 14th-century tombs inside the church. The chapel to the left of the high altar has a triptych by Matteo da Gualdo, depicting the *Madonna and Child* with *St. Peter* and *St. Vittorino* on either side. The relics of the latter saint are also here, perhaps because the abbey of San Pietro was an emanation of the foundation of San Vittorino. When it declined, the monastery of San Pietro became its heir and transferred the relics of the martyr to its own church.

Externally the church of San Pietro is distinguished by a lovely rectangular **facade** of 1268.

The lower zone is very linear with the large central portal soberly decorated with a band of vine scrolls and two small doors at the sides simply set flush with the wall. Two lions in stone flank the principal entrance.

The upper zone is richer, with three rose windows with ornaments on the columned spokes and the splayed frames.

Blind arcading is set between the lower and the upper parts and also terminates the top of the facade.

Above: the Abbey of San Pietro, with on the facing page the fine portal with its vine scrolls watched over by lions.

Amongst the rocks, basilicas, churches and steep streets, time seems to have stopped in Assisi. Vast plains stretch from the feet of the Franciscan Basilica.

THE UNIQUE ATMOSPHERE OF ASSISI

Wandering through the city we often encounter unexpected panoramic views, the remains of ancient monuments, small medieval churches, craft shops with objects in wrought iron, embroidery, pottery. This aspect of Assisi fascinates the pilgrims and visitors who come from all parts of the world throughout the year.
Pope John XXIII, a pilgrim to Assisi on October 4, 1962, wondered why «God had given Assisi this enchanting nature, these art splendors, this charm of sanctity, which seems to hover in the air and which the pilgrim feels as something tangible». But, «the answer», he said, «is easy. It is so that through a common and universal language men may learn to know each other as brothers».

An aerial view of the town, dominated by the Cathedral of St. Rufino and the Basilica of St. Clare.
Left: the ancient Church of St. Stephen.

Opposite page: the mighty bulk of the Rocca Maggiore, with its fortifications.

And the current pope, John Paul II, in his second visit to the city on March 12, 1982, added: «This is the second time I come to Assisi. And believe me, the emotions are the same, for here one breathes a unique atmosphere of a pure Christian faith and high human values of civilization. The two components, in fact, are here perfectly fused in the name of Francis and while they undoubtedly constitute one of the major glories of the history of Italy and its noble people, they have also had universal resonance, for the religious and civil development of a goodly number of countries on the earth has benefitted to some extent».

THE ROCCA MAGGIORE

The Rocca Maggiore stands on the crest of the hill which dominates Assisi. An old feudal stronghold, it probably dates to Lombard times. It was almost totally destroyed in 1198 by the inhabitants of the city (Francis was here then too, eighteen years old) when they rose up against imperial power and brought an end to the German dominion which had begun in 1173 with the occupation of the city by the Archbishop of Mainz and constituted a communal government in Assisi. Frederick II of Swabia lived here as a boy for several years, an orphan under the guardianship of Innocent III who entrusted him to Corrado of Lutzen, duke of Spoleto and imperial vicar, whose headquarters were here.

The fortress as it is now was rebuilt in 1367 for Cardinal Egidio Albornoz and enlarged between the 15th and 16th centuries with the erection of the polygonal tower and the smaller cylindrical one near the entrance.

At the end of the 14th century Ser Biordo Michelotti, gonfalonier of Assisi, strengthened the keep where his coat of arms can still be seen at the level of the third story. In the middle of the 15th century Piccinino had the Comacine masters work on the dodecagonal tower where they carved their ensign at the base. Pius II also had work done on the same tower – his coat of arms and the date 1460 are there. Urbano Vergerio, under the pontificate of Sixtus

IV, had the vaults renewed. Lastly Paul II, in 1535, had the entrance tower on the circular ramparts, where his coat of arms is to be found, reinforced.

In the following centuries the Rocca was used as a prison and gradually fell into neglect. The city of Assisi bought it in 1888.

The trapezoidal encircling walls, with a square tower at each corner, are connected to the city walls by a guard walk that terminates in a large twelve-sided tower. In the center is the Rocca, also square in plan and reinforced at the southeast corner by the tall keep.

This compact mighty ensemble still emanates an impression of warlike power and despite the various readaptations it is still a significant example of 14th-century military architecture.

The entire structure evokes the rivalry between the pope and the emperor, between Assisi and Perugia, between the «maiores» and the «minores» (aristocracy and the common people) – in which the city was involved for centuries.

But apart from these historical recollections, the heights on which the Rocca stands provide a unique observation point with a sweeping view of the entire Umbrian vale: from east to west one can see Mt. Subasio and all the towns in the plain from Spoleto to Perugia. Behind it is a steep gorge with the river Tescio at the bottom. On the height to the right of the Rocca Maggiore is the «Rocca Minore» or Small Fort, dating to more recent times and a defensive military outpost. St. Francis is universally

known and loved as a man of peace and non-violence, brother of all men and poet of the world of nature. The presence in Assisi of the Fort and the city walls might give the visitor a different impression, that of a warlike city.

When Francis was born in 1182, Italy was rent by fratricidal struggles: the «*minores*» were opposed to the «*maiores*», the communes were battling each other; civil and ecclesiastic authorities were engaged in a contest for power... And it is just this uneasy terrain on which Francis' vocation as peace-maker matured. With first-hand experience of the sufferings of war and the negative effects of hate and division, he became deeply convinced of the need to bring the words of the Gospels to all with the message of «*pax et bonum*».

Even though it does so differently, the Rocca of Assisi launches a message of peace: the search for a fraternal way of existence, of thought, of life; the commitment to dialogue and a new approach to relations between individuals, peoples, nations.

On these pages: various views of Assisi and the Rocca Maggiore which dominates the town and plain from on high.

THE SURROUNDINGS

SANTA MARIA DEGLI ANGELI

In the plain of Assisi, about four kilometers from the historical center, is the basilica of Santa Maria degli Angeli after which the surrounding area is named. Inside is the chapel of the Porziuncola: a place deeply loved by St. Francis and in which God conceded him special graces.

Various pages in the story of Franciscan life were written around the chapel: in 1208, listening to the Gospel, Francis became more clearly aware of his vocation; in 1216, in a vision Francis obtained from Jesus himself the indulgence of the «Pardon of Assisi» which was then approved by Pope Honorius III; in 1221 the famous Chapter «delle Stuoie» (of the mats) was enacted here, with the presence of about 5000 friars; in 1226 Francis died here singing the praises of sister death.

This is why St. Francis admonished his brothers never to abandon this blessed spot: «See to it my Brothers that you never leave this place; if you are thrust out on one side, enter again by the other; for truly this place is holy, and the dwelling of Christ and the Virgin His mother. It was here that, when we were few, the Most High multiplied us; here He made the soul of His poor shine with the light of wisdom; here He kindled our wills with the fire of His love. Here, whosoever prays with a devout heart, will obtain what he asks; but the offenses will be punished more severely. Therefore, my children, consider with reverence and honor this worthy place, as is fitting to the habitation of God particularly favored by Him and His Mother» (FF n. 1780).

Initially the **«Porziuncola»** was a chapel, built long before, and surrounded by a small grove (which may lie at the origin of the name – small portion) that belonged to the Benedictines of the monastery of San Benedetto on Mt. Subasio. It had been abandoned for a long time and Francis restored it and had it in «rent» from Abbot Teobaldo. After the death of the Saint various small buildings arose around the little church: the friars' choir, a number of small oratories and then a small convent.

In the second half of the 16th century Pius V ordered the construction of a great basilica to enclose and protect the Porziuncola and shelter the great crowds of pilgrims who continuously came. The building, on a design by the Perugino Galeazzo Alessi, was begun in 1568 and finished in 1684.

This vast imposing construction in classical style is dominated by an elegant dome visible from far off rising up over the surrounding plain.

As a basilica it is one of the largest in the world, 116 m long and with a maximum width of 65 meters.

The tripartite **interior** is empty with twelve side chapels embellished with frescoes and altarpieces by various artists from the 16th to the 20th century.

Beginning at the right, on entering is: the *Chapel of St. Anthony Abbot*, with works by Giorgetti and other Umbrian painters; the *Chapel of St. John Baptist*, with paintings by Giorgetti and Sermei; the *Chapel of St. Anne*, with works by Pomarancio and others; the *Chapel of St. Pius V*, with paintings by Martelli; the *Chapel of the Nativity* with works by various artists; the *altar of St. Peter*, with works by Mattei and others.

Beginning on the left, entering, is: the *Chapel of St. Diego d'Alcalà*, with paintings by various 17th and 18th-century artists; the *Chapel of the Stigmata*, with paintings by Giorgetti and Sermei; the *Chapel of St. Massimino*, with paintings by various artists; the *Chapel of the Incoronata*, with paintings on canvas by Simone Ciburri, 17th century; the *Chapel of the Madonna of the Rosary*, with 18th century works of the school of Conca; the *altar of the Holy Cross*, in polychrome marble, 1700.

Other works which enrich the Basilica in addition to many recent additions are the wooden *choir stalls* and a *pulpit* made by a group of friars, under the direction of Fra Luigi Selci, from 1698 to 1701; the *sacristy*, with carved walnut presses, by Fra Giacomo of Borgo San Sepolcro.

The **exterior** of the basilica was remodelled several times: after the earthquake of 1832, which seriously damaged the entire church, and once more in 1926-27 by the architect Cesare Bazzani. At the top of the tympanum is the bronze statue of the *Madonna* (7.15 m high) by the sculptor G. Colasanti, of 1930. The dome, built right over the small church of the Porziuncola, and designed by Galeazzo Alessi, rests on a polygonal base and terminates with a lantern on which the cross is set. Next to the dome (75 m high) is a Renaissance bell-tower.

Outside, to the left of the sanctuary is the **fountain with twenty-six jets** commissioned by the Medicis to quench the thirst of the pilgrims who came to take advantage of the indulgence of pardon.

INTERIOR OF THE PORZIUNCOLA

The «Porziuncola» was the third church St. Francis restored, after San Damiano and San Pietro della Spina, the result of hearing the voice of the Crucifix of San Damiano.

The interior of the Porziuncola preserves its original freshness intact. Even though we do not know exactly what Francis did, it is not difficult to imagine what the small works of restoration and consolidation were.

The walls were never painted and the stones are as they were so many centuries ago. At the center is an altar for the celebration of the Eucharist. On the altar the painting by Ilario da Viterbo: below, on the right, the *Miracle of the Roses*, and Francis, accompanied by two angels, going towards the Porziuncola; at the top, the *Apparition of Christ and the Madonna*, surrounded by a throng of angels, with Francis kneeling before the altar: below, left: Francis surrounded by bishops announces the privilege of the Pardon from the pulpit and, above, the Saint before Pope Honorius II imploring the confirmation of the indulgence. The painting dates to 1393.

On the facade of the chapel is a fresco by G. Federico Overbeck (1829) representing Francis invoking Jesus and the Madonna to obtain the gift of indulgence.

The simplicity and poverty of the spot are an invitation to discover the great wealth of the gift of peace and reconciliation.

The Porziuncola and its interior.

CHAPEL OF THE TRANSITO

A few meters from the Porziuncola, on the right side, in the apse of the basilica, is the chapel of the Transito (death). This was the infirmary of the original convent, one of the huts scattered through the grove, that the friars built to live in. St. Francis spent the last hours of his earthly existence here and died after having himself placed on the bare earth the evening of October 3, 1226.

A fresco by Domenico Bruschi (1886) on the outer wall depicts the *Death of St. Francis*, surrounded by friars and Jacopa dei Settesoli.

On the interior walls, Giovanni Spagna (1520) frescoed the figures of some of Francis' first companions: Bernardo, Ginepro, Silvestro, Masseo, Leone, Egidio.

Above the altar, in a reliquary, the girdle used by the Saint.

Behind the altar is a tender melancholy statue of *St. Francis* in glazed terracotta by Andrea della Robbia (1490). He holds the Gospels and the Cross.

Another fine work by Della Robbia is the six-panel polyptych showing *Francis receiving the stigmata* and various scenes regarding the birth of Christ. It is in the crypt (to be reached from the right arm of the transept) which was recently built near the old foundations of the original convent.

Above: the old Convent. At the side: the Chapel of the Transito.

CONVENT MUSEUM

Some of the rooms on the ground floor of the convent house the «Museo della Porziuncola», with its precious collection of church vestments and fine paintings, including a *Cross* by Giunta Pisano (perhaps dating to 1236) and a 13th-century portrait of *St. Francis* (by the so-called St. Francis Master). The Saint stands majestically holding the cross and an open book on which is written «*Hic mihi viventi lectus fuit et morienti*» (Here was my rest in life and in death).

Other interesting pictures are a *Madonna* by Sano di Pietro, the *Madonna and Child* by Mezzastris, and various 16th-century paintings.

A missionary ethnographic museum is installed in other more recent rooms.

From the museum access is had to the «dormitory of S. Bernardino», so called after the saint who had it finished. It consists of seventeen small cells furnished with period pieces and other precious memoirs (manuscripts, paintings, prints, various household objects). This is all that rests of the old convent.

Left: Saint Bonaventura by Tiberio d'Assisi; facing page, above: the Della Robbia tabernacle with the Coronation of the Virgin; below, left: St. Francis by the «St. Francis Master» (13th cent.); right: the Crucifix by Giunta Pisano (first half of the 13th cent.).

THE ROSETO

Various sites that occupy the area where the original «roseto» once stood go by the name of «roseto» or rose garden. They all have to do with the daily life of St. Francis and of the friars: prayer, dialogue, love for God's creatures, penitence.

Access is from the basilica through a courtyard built in 1882. At the beginning is a statue of *St. Francis with the Doves*. At the center of the rose garden is a bronze monument by Vincenzo Rosignoli (1916), *St. Francis and the Lamb*. On the base of the statue are various scenes from the Canticle of the Creatures.

All around the «thornless roses».

One winter night St. Francis was praying in his cell when he was tempted to abandon the life he had undertaken. To overcome this temptation he undressed and threw himself into a patch of briars near the cell. When they touched him, the thorns disappeared and a garden of thornless roses sprang into bloom.

Next to the garden is the rose-garden chapel, an oratory where the Saint used to pray or rest. The chapel and the grotto were built by St. Bonaventura in the 13th century and later enlarged in the 15th century by St. Bernardino of Siena.

The walls of the chapel are decorated with frescoes by Tiberio of Assisi (1506-1516): *St. Francis and his first companions; Franciscan saints;* the *Miracle of the Roses;* the *Story of the concession of the indulgence of the Pardon of Assisi.*

Above, left: the statue of St. Francis and the doves; right: the spineless roses of St. Francis; at the side: the Saint with a lamb, bronze statue by Vincenzo Rosignoli.

SAN DAMIANO

The Sanctuary of San Damiano, in which remembrances of St. Francis and St. Clare go hand in hand, lies in the midst of the green olive groves around Assisi.

Situated outside the city walls and set against the hill on which Assisi rises, the small church was built as a chapel between the 7th and the 8th century, in a rustic style, meant to be used simply as a point for prayer by whoever might be in the surroundings. At the beginning of the 13th century it was pratically abandoned. Although a priest was supposedly responsible for the structure, no one bothered to restore it since it was so little use to the religious community.

Francis began to go there shortly after he turned twenty and was passionately seeking for the meaning of life. After he heard the voice of the Crucifix which told him to repair the Church, he set about rebuilding it. From that time on the chapel became for him a central reference point in his new experience of life. When Clare wanted to follow his example, St. Francis gave her this spot where she lived for forty-two years until August 11, 1253 when she left this earthly life for that in heaven. Francis returned here several times. It was in these surroundings that in 1225, having received the stigmata and almost blind, he composed in unified form *The Canticle of the Creatures*, a marvelous expression of love for God, for men, and for God's creatures.

When the Poor Clares left in 1260, the place remained as it was until the 16th century when the Friars Minor built the cloister and enlarged the convent. After the suppression of the holdings of the church in 1860, San Da-

miano was bought by the Englishman Lord Ripon. After more than a century, in 1983, his heirs donated the property to the church and the convent to the Curia Generalizia of the Brothers Minor.

Currently it houses a small community of Friars Minor and also the novices. These young people who desire to embrace the Franciscan life spend a year here studying both Franciscan spirituality and verifying their choice of vocation.

In San Damiano, art is «mute», religious feeling of primary importance. Poverty, simplicity, peace reign sovereign. Many of the pages of Franciscan life, as described in the early biographies of the Saint, here still seem to belong to the present. The spirit of St. Francis and of St. Clare lives on.

A simple portico serves as entrance to San Damiano. In the square there is a shrine with 15th-century frescoes of Sienese school (the *Madonna and Child between St. Francis, St. Rufino, St. Clare, St. Damian*). To the right of the church is the **Chapel of St. Jerome** with frescoes by Tiberio of Assisi (1517): the *Virgin Enthroned, St. Francis and St. Clare, St. Jerome and St. Bernardine*. Next to them *St. Sebastian and St. Rocco*.

The Sanctuary of San Damiano, original complex situated in the surroundings of Assisi.

The **inside of the church** is simple, enveloped in shadows, an invitation to prayer. On the altar is a copy of the *Crucifix* which ordered St. Francis to repair His house (the 12th-century original is in the Basilica of Santa Chiara). In the apse is a fresco in Byzantine style with the Madonna and Child between St. Rufino and St. Damian. At the back is a small choir (stalls) of the early 16th century.

In a chapel to the right of the church is the wooden *Crucifix* by Fra Innocenzo da Palermo, of 1637: the expression on the face of Christ changes according to the angle of observation. It can be smiling, suffering, dying.

The entrance to the small **Choir of St. Clare** is to the right of the wooden choir. The stalls, the backs, the lecterns are still those from the time of St. Clare. The names of the first Poor Clares are listed on a parchment. When Gabriele D'Annunzio visited this spot he noted: «...I go down five steps into the choir of St. Clare, the choir of our Lady of Poverty. The backs are made of boards joined together haphazardly like the planks of those life rafts the ship's carpenters built with good-sized firs in the tumult of shipwreck. The seats and the door of a parapet in front

are made of barely smoothed planks. The lectern is held on a pine cone set in a squared log...».

It is the visible expression of their devotion to extreme poverty.

A narrow flight of stairs leads up to the **Garden of St. Clare**, a suggestive spot from which to admire the valley below. Here St. Francis composed the *Canticle of the Creatures* in its entirety. Still further up is a small frescoed chapel known as **St. Clare's oratory**, which in turn leads to the **dormitory** where the Poor Clares slept. Here St. Clare lived her moments of greatest suffering and pain, here she was visited by Pope Innocent IV, here she died. On the altar is a 15th-century wooden *Crucifix* by an anonymous artist.

An internal staircase leads down into the **cloister**.

The internal cloister of San Damiano has retained all its simplicity. It is still a corner of peace and silence. There are two frescoes by Eusebio Perugino (1507) on the part next to the church: the *Annunciation* and *St. Francis Receiving the Stigmata*.

At the back of the cloister is the **Refectory of the Poor Clares**, with the old tables of early times. This is where the sisters ate their frugal meals. A vase of flowers on the last table to the right marks the place where St. Clare generally sat. Pope Gregory IX was a guest of the Poor Clares in 1228 and imposed the blessing of the meal on St. Clare: the sign of the cross was impressed on each loaf of bread.

There are various frescoes by Dono Doni on the walls. Above the refectory is another wing of the old monastery with the cell of St. Agnes, St. Clare's sister.

Facing page: two views of the cloister of San Damiano; above: the rustic Choir stalls of St. Clare.

ABBEY OF SAN BENEDETTO

The abbey of San Benedetto lies on the slope of Mt. Subasio in a marvelous panoramic position. From Assisi it can be reached by the road that begins at Via Madonna dell'Ulivo, about 500 meters from Porta Nuova, or by the road that begins somewhat above the Carceri.

There is a scarcity of documents which might help us to trace the history of this abbey, founded by the Marchigian monks of Farfa perhaps as early as the 9th century. It was the principal headquarters for monasticism in Assisi, and could house up to forty monks. After a period of flourishing life, monasticism died out towards the end of the 14h century. St. Francis often came here and it was the abbot of San Benedetto who let him use the Porziuncola in return for an annual rent of a basket of fish.

The strategic position of the monastery made it a ready refuge for those who had left during the fratricidal struggles in Assisi. In April of 1399 the mercenaries of Broglia, in view of the dangers inherent in the site, decreed that it be demolished. The monastery was left to itself and abandoned and what remained passed to private hands.

Thanks to the enterprise of the monks of the other abbey of Assisi, San Pietro, the extant structures were bought in 1945 and gradually restored with state intervention. Most of the old abbey can now once more be enjoyed by the public.

The perimetral walls, the **facade** of the church in Romanesque style, the semicircular apse, some of the rooms in the monastery and two fine **crypts** still furnish an idea of its original splendor. One of the crypts dates to the 11th century and is Romanesque in style with a cruciform ground plan and eight monolithic columns that support the arches and beautiful Romanesque capitals. The other crypt, which saw the light after the most recent archaeological excavations, may date to the 9th century and is called the «triastyle» crypt for it has three monolithic columns.

Facing page, above: the path near San Damiano and, below, the Refectory of the Poor Clares in the Sanctuary, with St. Clare's place marked by a vase of flowers. Above: the 16th-century fresco with the Madonna, the Child and Saint in the left chapel of San Damiano and San Bonaventura's Cross.

EREMO DELLE CARCERI
(Hermitage)

Hidden in the dense woods of holm-oaks, on Mt. Subasio, about 800 meters above sea level, is the Eremo delle Carceri or Hermitage: a place of peace and silence, where the impact of Franciscan spirituality is still fresh and immediate. This is where Francis and his first companions withdrew in prayer every so often. The present small convent structure then grew up around the original nucleus. The convent was first restructured by St. Bernardino of Siena in the 15th century, later enlarged to its current forms in the 16th and 17th centuries. It is all built against the rock out of which many parts have been hollowed. Originally a small oratory dedicated to the Madonna, «Santa Maria delle Carceri» (carcere or prison here means retreat), it belonged to the city of Assisi which first assigned it to the Benedictines and then to the Franciscans.

Facing page, above: the complex of the Abbey of San Benedetto; below: the interior of the crypt in the abbey. Above: the Eremo delle Carceri (Hermitage).

What meditation and contemplation really mean becomes clear in the course of a quiet visit.
The entrance leads into the small **cloister**, with a well at the center. On the left, below, is the **refectory**, and above, the **dormitory** with its small cells. Across is the **church** with its small open bell tower. Inside to be noted are the *altar* and a small *choir* for prayer. Entrance to the **Chapel of Santa Maria delle Carceri** is from here. Under the church is the **grotto of St. Francis** with the stone he used as bed. This is where St. Francis prayed and fasted, wept, and discoursed with God. Before leaving, note the «devil's hole», into which the devil sank when he was driven out by the Saint.
Outside, next to age-old trees, is a monument by Vincenzo Rosignoli (1926) – a bronze sculpture representing *St. Francis receiving two doves from a young man.*
Before continuing on into the woods to see the various caves used for prayer, note the bed of a torrent that dried up at the Saint's command for he did not want the sound of the water to disturb the friars in their prayers.
Near the bridge is the **Chapel of St. Mary Magdalen**, of the 15th century, containing the mortal remains of Fra Barnaba Manassei of Terni, who invented the pawn-shop (Monti di Pietà) in 1462 to help the poor of Perugia.
At the Carceri nature reigns sovereign.
Various paths lead to the top of Mt. Subasio (1290 m. high), thought by some to be a former volcano. The vegetation on the mountain consists of olives (below), woods (center), fields (at the top).

Left: the Grotto of St. Francis, where the Saint withdrew to meditate; below: the hermitage enveloped in the green woods in a gorge of Mt. Subasio. Facing page: the lovely cloister.

RIVOTORTO

Rivotorto takes its name from a tortuous stream which descends from the slopes of Mt. Subasio and crosses this stretch of the plain of Assisi on its way to the river Ose and the Tiber.

On his way back from Rome where Innocent III had given him oral approval of the Rule, St. Francis stopped here with his first brothers for about two years in 1209-1210.

The «hovel», enclosed in the current **Sanctuary**, is witness to the place and the simple poor life style of the original group of friars. The dwelling consisted of two rooms, one for sleeping and one for eating, separated by a small chapel. The friars had to leave because a local peasant needed the rooms. From here they went to the Porziuncola. But this was not the end of Rivotorto. Some of them continued to live here and the devotion to the Saint was more alive than ever.

In 1586 the hovel was covered by a vast church that was destroyed by an earthquake and rebuilt in NeoGothic style in its present forms in 1854. In 1926 the «hovel» was declared a national monument.

Inside the church are twelve paintings on canvas by Cesare Sermei (1600), depicting *Scenes from the life of St. Francis*. A mosaic by G. Conti (1955) glitters on the facade of the sanctuary. It depicts two episodes that took place at Rivotorto: St. Francis appearing to his friars on a chariot of fire; and a friar warning the Emperor Ottone IV who is passing through, of the fragility of earthly grandeur.

Below: the Sanctuary of Rivotorto; facing page: two views of the Hovel of St. Francis inside the sanctuary.

THE CHRONICLE OF A CATASTROPHE

September 26th 1997 will remain a painfully memorable date in the age-long history of Assisi. In fact, on the morning of that day, at 11.42 a.m., after a night in which the stability of many buildings was sorely tested by a strong earthquake, a new, more violent tremor tore the ancient and most sacred heart of the city of St. Francis. All the main monuments, from the Cathedral of Saint Rufino to the Basilica of Saint Clare, from Santa Maria degli Angeli to the Sanctuary of Saint Damian, were seriously damaged and declared unfit for use.

However, the real tragedy took place in the Saint's Upper Basilica where, in the late morning, an inspection was being carried out by technicians from the Monuments and Fine Arts Office, accompanied by some monks and the chief city authorities, in order to verify the damage caused by the night's tremors.

This new earthquake had a devastating effect on the Upper Basilica, causing the collapse of part of the vault which, crumbling into a huge cloud of dust, overwhelmed those present, killing two technicians and two monks.

THE LOST MASTERPIECES

In those terrible moments, in addition to some fragments of the elegant starry sky painted on an intense blue background, one of the sections of the famous Doctors' Vault, where St. Jerome was frescoed, was lost. Also lost was a section of the intrados of the counter-façade, where the figures of St. Rufino, St. Anthony, St. Francis and St. Clare, amongst others, were depicted, as well as the St. Matthew on the Evangelists' Vault, decorated by Cimabue

An image of the damage caused by the violent earthquake on September 26th 1997, and the scaffolding erected to make it possible for the long and difficult restoration work. Below: the vault of the transept, decorated by Cimabue and at present partially collapsed (the photo shoes the lost section) as it was before the earthquake.

above the transept which, as it fell, irremediably crushed the splendid high altar. On the ground there remained the desolate spectacle of debris, on which technicians, restoration experts and art historians feverishly began to intervene immediately, urged on by a wave of emotion which spread throughout the world. Thus began the painstaking process of restoration, destined to be a long task, with an impassioned search for fragments in order to put together an authentic artistic puzzle, with the help of pictures of the once splendid frescoes.

This was, perhaps, the first sign of the difficult process of rebirth, pursued with an unshakable determination, while the earth tremors continued for several months and necessary interventions, often demanding and radical, were planned for all the churches, basilicas and buildings in the city. Wounded Assisi returned to normal life, albeit with difficulty, and while expert and enthusiastic hands tried to put back together the stupendous frescoes of what had always been its symbol, the city forced itself to shine again with its ancient, albeit now impaired, splendor.

The splendid frescoes by Giotto which, after the devastating earthquake, it will no longer be possible to admire: St. Jerome on the Doctors' Vault, and the portraits of St. Anthony, St. Benedict, St. Peter Martyr and St. Dominic, frescoed on the intrados of the counter-façade. Below: images showing the difficult restoration work to be carried out, with great care and dedication, by expert and enthusiastic professionals.

PRAYERS

If the visit to the city of Assisi has filled you with joy, prayer can enrich you still further, filling your heart with God. Francis, as Tommaso da Celano says, «was not so much a man praying, as he was a man who had himself become a prayer». For prayer expressed the unbroken continuity of his relationship with God. Prayer was therefore expectation, desire, encounter, listening, possession, repose, nostalgia, search, praise, joy, thanksgiving, dialogue. A variegated reality, which was basically nothing but the expression of a profound colloquium between a man and his God.

We wish to terminate this book by citing some of the loveliest prayers composed by St. Francis, in the hopes that his charm will be contagious and chellange you to repeat the same experience of prayer.

THE CANTICLE OF THE CREATURES

Most high omnipotent good Lord,
   to Thee Praise, glory, honour, and every benediction.
To Thee alone Most High do they belong.
   And no man is worthy to pronounce Thy Name.
Praise be to Thee my Lord with all Thy creatures.
   Especially for Master Brother Sun
   Who illuminates the day for us,
   And Thee Most High he manifests.
Praise be to Thee my Lord
   for Sister Moon and for the stars,
   In Heaven Thou hast formed them, shining, precious, fair.
Praise be to Thee my Lord for Brother Wind,
   For air and clouds, clear sky and all the weathers
   Through which Thou sustainest all Thy creatures.
Praise be to Thee my Lord for Sister Water.
   She is useful and humble, precious and pure.
Praise be to Thee my Lord for Brother Fire,
   Through him our night Thou dost enlighten,
   And he is fair and merry, boisterous and strong.
Praise be to Thee my Lord for our sister Mother Earth,
   Who nourishes and sustains us all,
   Bringing forth divers fruits, and many colored flowers and herbs.
Praise be to Thee my Lord for those who pardon grant for love of Thee
   And bear infirmity and tribulation,
   Blessed be those who live in peace,
   For by Thee Most High they shall be crowned.
Praise be to Thee my Lord for our Sister Bodily Death
   From whom no living man can flee;
   Woe to them who die in mortal sin
   But blessed they who shall be found in Thy most holy Will
   To them the second death can do no harm.
O bless and praise my Lord all creatures,
   And thank and serve Him in deep humility.

(Fonti Francescane, n. 263)

PRAISE OF THE LORD

Thou art the holy Lord God, Thou art God, of gods,
Who only workest marvels.
Thou art strong. Thou art great. Thou art most high.
Thou art almighty. Thou art the holy Father, King of heaven and earth.
Thou art threefold and one; Lord God of gods.
Thou art good, every good, the highest good.
The Lord God living and true.
Thou art love, Thou art charity. Thou art wisdom.
Thou art humility. Thou art patience.
Thou art beauty. Thou art security. Thou art rest.
Thou art joy and gladness. Thou art our hope.
Thou art justice. Thou art temperance.
Thou art all our wealth and plenty.
Thou art beauty. Thou art gentleness. Thou art the protector.
Thou art the keeper and defender.
Thou art our refuge and strength.
Thou art our faith. Thou art our hope.
Thou art our charity. Thou art our sweetness.
Thou art our eternal life.
Great and wonderful Lord, God almighty, loving and merciful Saviour.

(Fonti Francescane, n. 261)

COMMENT TO THE LORD'S PRAYER

OUR FATHER: creator, redeemer, our consoler and Saviour.

WHO ART IN HEAVEN: in the angels and in the saints, illuminating them so they will know that Thou, Lord art light; inflaming them to love, because Thou, Lord, art love; living in them, the fullness of their joy, for Thou, Lord, art the Highest Good, eternal, from which all good comes, without which there is no good.

HALLOWED BE THY NAME: let our knowledge of Thee become clearer in us, so that we may see the fullness of Thy benefices, the extension of Thy promises, the heights of Thy majesty, the depths of Thy judgement.

THY KINGDOM COME: so that Thou mayest reign in us by means of grace and Thou makest us to reach Thy kingdom where there is a vision of Thee without shadows, a perfect love, a happy union, eternal enjoyment.

THY WILL BE DONE IN HEAVEN AS IT IS ON EARTH: so that we may love Thee with all our hearts thinking always of Thee; with all our souls, always desiring Thee, with all our minds, turning to Thee all our attentions and in all things seeking Thy honor. And with all our forces, spending all our energies and feelings of soul and body in the service of Thy love and for naught else; and so that we may love our neighbor as we love ourselves, drawing all with all our power to Thy love, enjoying the fortunes of others as if they were ours and pitying them in their misfortunes and bearing offense to none.

GIVE US OUR DAILY BREAD: Thy most beloved Son, our Lord Jesus Christ.

GIVE US THIS DAY: in remembrance and reverent comprehension of that love He had for us and all He said, did, and suffered for us.

AND FORGIVE US OUR DEBTS: in Thy ineffable mercy, in virtue of the passion of Thy Son and for the intercession and the merits of the Blessed Virgin Mary and of all Thy saints.

AS WE FORGIVE OUR DEBTORS: and that which we are unable to fully pardon, Thou, Lord, make us fully pardon, so that, for Thy sake, we can truly love our enemies and we can devoutly intercede for them with Thee, and let no one render evil for evil, and let all seek to be of aid to all in Thee.

AND LEAD US NOT INTO TEMPTATION: hidden or manifest, sudden or inexistent.

AND DELIVER US FROM EVIL: past, present and future. Amen.

(Fonti Francescane, nn. 266-274)

CONTENTS